Finding Grace

To Joanie —
May you find grace
in all you do.
Shirlee Taylor Haizlip
Feb 21, 2004

Also by Shirlee Taylor Haizlip

The Sweeter the Juice: A Family Memoir in Black and White

In the Garden of Our Dreams: Memoirs of a Marriage
(with Harold C. Haizlip)

Finding Grace

Two Sisters and
the Search for Meaning
Beyond the Color Line

Shirlee Taylor Haizlip

*f*P
Free Press
New York London Toronto Sydney

Free Press
A Division of Simon & Schuster, Inc.
1230 Avenue of the Americas
New York, NY 10020

Copyright © 2004 by Shirlee Taylor Haizlip
All rights reserved,
including the right of reproduction
in whole or in part in any form.

FREE PRESS and colophon are trademarks of Simon & Schuster, Inc.

For information regarding special discounts for bulk purchases,
please contact Simon & Schuster Special Sales at 1-800-456-6798
or business@simonandschuster.com

Designed by Nancy Singer Olaguera

Manufactured in the United States of America

1 3 5 7 9 10 8 6 4 2

Library of Congress Cataloging-in-Publication Data is available.

ISBN 0-7432-0053-5

Permissions appear on pages 271–72.

Acknowledgments

It has been a long and winding journey to bring this book to fruition. Foremost I thank my husband, Harold, for walking beside me, behind me, and in front of me, and holding me up. His insights, kindness, and compassion are the foundations of this project. I am so very grateful for the support and assistance of my daughters, Deirdre and Melissa, in completing all the necessary work. They were my personal two-woman cheering squad.

Special thanks to my sister Jewelle and her husband, Jim Gibbs, who urged me to the finish line. Thanks to my friend, mentor, and West Coast mother, Libby Clark, who made sure I stayed focused. I could not have completed the book without the grace and comfort of some very special friends, including Marcia Alessi, Joan Benson, Joyce Black, Ruth Boldt, John Caragozian, Anne Combs, Diana Edmonds, Joyce Forn, Dennee Frey, Phyllis Fields, Dr. Pearl Grimes, Kinderly Haskins, Patty Hill, Melody Jackson, Kay Lachter, Suz Landay, Rosie Lyske, Michele Maddox, Marcia Mosebay, Louise Nalli, Kelley Nelson, Denise Nicholas, Kate Nunes, Carrie Perry, Marian Randall, Patricia Rye, Devon Sedlacek, Ramona Selby, Julia Soto, Victoria Swackenberg, Phyllis Tobin, Mary Thompson, Shahen Varden, and Dr. William Young.

To my longtime friend, Wilbert Howard, and to the "best and brightest" of my Ansonia High School classmates, James Hallihan, James Mongillo, Robert Mueller, and William Ruddy, I extend special thanks for their affection, wisdom, and insights during an unforgettable voyage down Alaska's Inside Passage.

Thanks to my friends at American Heritage.

A special thank you to all those who wrote letters that appear in the book and to those whose letters meant so much but for which there was not enough space.

Without the public relations wizardry of Courtney Fischer, many eyes might not have seen this book. Wylie O'Sullivan pulled all the necessary strings to move the project along.

And to all the rest of my family members and special friends who took my pulse, checked my temperature, and oversaw my "vitals," I am especially grateful.

My agent, Faith Childs, has been wonderful during the gestation period of this book. It is always comforting to know that she is there. Finally, I owe much to the book's godfather and guiding spirit, my editor, Dominick Anfuso.

Shirlee Taylor Haizlip
Los Angeles, October 1, 2003

To my mother—
who found hope, love, and Grace

Contents

PART I

*When the Rainbow
Is Not Enough*

PROLOGUE

After packing hurriedly in Connecticut, my mother flew into Los Angeles at the end of a cool January in 1998. Early the next evening we drove down to Brea, a small town edged with the suede brown mountains characteristic of Southern California. She began to cry as she entered the building. A professionally somber official ushered us to a pleasantly lit, immaculate area painted in neutral tones.

My mother stood in the quiet, carpeted room looking down at a mirror image of herself in a white coffin. Not exactly a mirror image, since the dead woman, my ninety-five-year-old Aunt Grace, was eight years older than my mother with just a few more wrinkles. Crying steadily but quietly, my mother, now tiny with age, patted her sister's hand, saying over and over again, "We only had six years together. We only had six years together."

Jeff Scott, the dead woman's grandson; Harold, my husband; and I were the only other ones at the viewing at that time. In the end, few of Grace's white extended family were there to say a final good-bye. Most likely because they lived in far distant places. They had drifted apart. They exchanged Christmas cards but otherwise had little time for the details of their separate lives.

It was her black family, the family she had left, the family that she had forgotten, the family that had returned to her, that gathered to mourn. It was the black family that joined her son-in-law and grandchildren in grieving for her. Not exactly the usual suspects. Not exactly a Hollywood ending for a poignant story of high drama.

Like thousands of others who passed for white in America, Grace left her home in Washington, D.C., moved around a lot, settled in Cleveland, and finally retired in Orange County, California to be near her only daughter, son-in-law, and grandchildren. There she had lived a shielded life, a life that only she knew was compromised. It was a life that precluded close friends and eliminated questions about her literally dark past.

As we paid our respects, it occurred to me that some might say we were assuming the traditional role of the good black, the noble black, the all-forgiving mammy who, no matter how she had been treated, proudly demonstrated her loyalty at the end.

Was it true? Had we become someone else's balm in Gilead once again? Or had we truly reached across that gulf we call race in America and come together as a family, to do the things that families must do? It was clear to me that nobility had nothing to do with our feelings. My mother had lost her only sister, whom she had so recently found. I had lost the aunt I had so deeply wanted to recover. Ours were the normal feelings of grief.

Families account for their internal dynamics in different ways. Two years before her death, Grace moved into a nursing home after she fell and broke her hip. Although she recovered and was of sound mind, she could not return to her home because she lived alone and it was felt she needed full-time coverage to ensure her safety and best interests. She died of pneumonia in that nursing home. Her death was quick to come.

Around the receiving room at the funeral home, on displays

that Jeff had made, my mother saw pictures of herself with Grace during their six-year reconnection. Each carefully constructed collage was a public acknowledgment of their sisterhood, of their coming from the same womb, of their sharing the same DNA.

On the face of it, it was simple, homey proof. Proof that could break your heart. Sweet, visual evidence that black and white were inextricably intertwined. Proof that black was white and white was black. Proof that family need not stop at the color line. Proof that the past is prologue to the present. Proof that dark family secrets have a way of working themselves into the communal light. Proof that the light can be warm and good and right.

The funeral took place the next day in the same facility, a muted, gabled building that looked like a colonial home in New England, my mother's part of the country. The presiding minister, who did not know my aunt, for she had no longer attended church, was intrigued and deeply moved by her life's story—and her sister's as well—as related by Jeff.

"Finding Grace" was the title the pastor chose for his eulogy. Its double meaning was profoundly resonant—and profoundly sad. Jeff, his two sisters, Laura and Lisa, Laura's husband, and my mother sat in the first-row family pew. Aside from my husband and our daughter, Melissa, a few friends of the grandchildren and son-in-law, and a neighbor, there were few other mourners. Perhaps that was as it should be.

Grace died as she had lived in later years, an almost solitary, white life. Her sister, although now too in a convalescent center, continues to live a black life. Race had transformed both their lives. With the publication of their story, an entire new set of life patterns came into play. In unexpected ways, the script changed. Much had to be ad-libbed. For all of us. On both sides.

And so we move on to ask the big questions. What happens in this country when those who thought of themselves as white, if they thought about it at all, learn of their additional genetic information, of their DNA ties to, as my colleague Stephen Carter puts it, "the darker nation"? How are these folk best described—"formerly white" or "allegedly white" or "still white with black heritage" or "mostly white" or "a little bit black" or "white, I think" or "touched by the brush" or "Heinz 57" or "Euro American and African American" or simply "American"? How did they receive us, and how did we assimilate them?

Inquiring minds have asked, What happened between your mother and her sister? Did they become friends? Did her sister call herself black? Did she ever explain why she chose to pass? Did your mother forgive her? Did you forgive her? How did all of the relatives you "found" react? Did they accept you? Did they accept themselves? Was there any hostility? Did any of them feel uncomfortable? What do they call themselves now? Do you keep in touch, doing the things that "real" family members do? How did the black part of the family react to the situation? Were any of those members angered or dismayed? Did this happen in many other families? Most of these questions will be addressed in the pages to come.

1

A Twice-Told Tale

A PASSING STORY

In her recently published autobiography, *Just Lucky, I Guess*, Carol Channing wrote what television promotional spots for a well-watched national show would later tout as "a shocking revelation."

It seems that on the eve of Carol's leaving home to attend Bennington College when she was sixteen, her mother told her that Carol's father had black heritage and had been born in Georgia, rather than in Providence, Rhode Island, as Carol had been led to believe. Her mother shared the information with her, she said, because she wanted Carol to know that she could very well have a child who looked colored.

Carol's paternal grandmother had been a black woman who had a baby with a white man. The baby was light skinned, and the mother fled the state, taking a job as a domestic in Providence. The circumstances of the mother's leaving were not offered, but one could assume that her remaining in the Deep South town with the white man's son was neither prudent nor safe.

At some point, young Channing "crossed over," as the vernacular was then, and passed for white. He attended Brown University on scholarship, served in the First World War as a white man, and returned to have a successful career in journalism. He became a Christian Scientist lecturer on the West Coast as a white man.

As a child, Carol remembers singing with her father songs she thought were hymns but later learned were gospel. Her father, she said, loved music, and the first Broadway show her parents took her to was the all-black production of *Green Pastures*.

Famed entertainer Ethel Waters became her son's "unofficial" grandmother. One of her best friends and frequent costars on the road was Louis Armstrong, and she appeared in a traveling show with Hines, Hines and Dad, the black family singing-and-dancing act out of which Gregory Hines would emerge a star. She reported that she often went to the Savoy Ballroom in Harlem "to learn the latest steps" and was usually the only white person there. It is clear that Carol Channing had a special affinity for black people.

When CNN television host Larry King asked Channing if her father were black, Channing, looking somewhat perplexed, said, "No, his skin was as white as mine." Like many people in America, Channing paired whiteness with race. In a circuitous few moments, King tried to pin Channing down about her racial history, but she deftly parried his inquiries. She said that she was part of the face of the new America. She admitted to being "proud" of her background and credited it with making her a successful singer and dancer. Demonstrating part of a dance routine, she said that "no white woman could have performed that arabesque" that she danced in the Broadway show *Hello, Dolly!* Carol included no pictures of her parents, grandmother, or son in her book.

For theater purists and historians, Channing opened a window they did not know existed: She, not Pearl Bailey, had actually been the first black Dolly in the 1960s production.

The Larry King segment suggested that if Channing had shared the story of her heritage early in her career it would have curtailed her future opportunities and she would not have become Carol Channing, the blond icon of *Hello, Dolly!, Thoroughly Modern Millie,* and *Gentlemen Prefer Blondes.* With its preference for "traditional casting," the American theater would not have accommodated Carol Channing, no matter how white her skin or skilled her dance steps.

My older sister Mauryne, the same age and coloring as Carol Channing, tried to make it in show business but was relegated to black plays and the black movies called "race films" because she refused to pass. In the few films where she was the female star, my sister looked like a pale white woman, surrounded by brown-skinned men. She played with the famous vaudevillian Flournoy Miller and with Mantan Moreland, who had a long run as the black chauffeur in the Charlie Chan series. Mauryne's forthrightness about her race penalized her and stunted her career.

The Channing revelation and the reaction to it are markers of how American society has changed, being willing to recognize that people other than those designated as black may be "part" this and "part" that. For some, at least, the "one drop of black blood" rule that for hundreds of years dictated on which side of the color line one could stand no longer applies.

I was and still am intrigued by the Channing story and its social implications. I discussed it with many of my white contemporaries. It was if they did not have the vocabulary to articulate their feelings or opinions about this racial shift of a famous person. Mentally, I footnoted the fact that few if any of them had had any kind of personal experience with passing. It was something they all had read about to varying degrees, or remembered from various expositions of the mulatto Julie's role in *Show Boat*.

One friend, a female, middle-aged producer of plays on Broadway and in regional theater, sort of shrugged her shoulders. "Well, no, Channing would not have gotten the parts she did if it had been known that she was black. Despite the way she looked. You know, the theater then was all about 'traditional casting,' and if you said 'black,' the minds of the directors, producers, and casting people would lock in on some stereotype. Carol would become ten shades darker in their minds." I pressed her. "Well, what can I say? Now, if it had been Elizabeth Taylor . . ."

On the other hand, "bemused" is how I felt about the casting of the not-quite-swarthy Anthony Hopkins, a white man, to play a black man who was passing for white in the film version of Philip Roth's novel *The Human Stain*. Hollywood producers found it a compelling enough story to make, but not compelling enough to use a light-skinned black actor in the leading role. It goes without saying that Hollywood was after the buck, and surely Anthony Hopkins, one of the silver screen's most accomplished and best-known luminaries, was a big draw. But still, wouldn't it have been wondrous to put a real, live potential passer in that role? One could argue on the other side, of course, that the producers were making the point that a white actor could indeed pass for a black man. It would seem that, in some circles at least, we have come a long way.

When I was growing up in Connecticut, one of my father's most sophisticated and exquisitely cultured friends was a light-skinned black man who resembled Anthony Hopkins. Having come to Bridgeport with his family from some Southern town, he worked as a high school teacher, although he was qualified to do other things. He was the only one in the family with pass-for-white skin. His wife was brown with curly hair, as were all his handsome children, save one. Each of his sons came to a bad end, two dying of unnatural causes and one in and out of mental institutions. The remaining child, a daughter, became a minister. I surmise now that life for that variegated colored family in the white Connecticut of the '40s must have been complicated.

Then there's the Thomas Jefferson drama, still unfolding. People often ask me how I feel about the reactions of the Jefferson family to the news of their kin of color. First, their story was old news to me. Many black Americans with roots in Washington, D.C., Virginia, or Maryland had grown up with the story, had accepted it as fact, and truly thought little about it. Both my parents told me about it when I was a little girl in the '30s, saying they also knew several other black descendents of various "first families of Virginia." In a certain black set in Washington, people were proud of their connections to the Virginia gentry or to Confederate Civil War heroes. The news was a shock only to white folk.

It is just a matter of time before the entire Jefferson clan will accept the inevitability of their extended family. Annette Gordon-Reed laid out the case of Jefferson's paternity of Sally

Hemings's children definitively in her brilliant book *Thomas Jefferson and Sally Hemings: An American Controversy*. For me, red-haired black people with Jefferson DNA make the argument moot. When I was on my book tour, a descendent of Sally Hemings came out to hear me speak. He later introduced himself to me, and I trembled as I looked into the piercing eyes of Thomas Jefferson that sat above his hooked nose.

Every week, it seems a new revelation colors our white icons. Virginie Amélie Gautreau, the haughty subject of John Singer Sargent's *Madame X*, painted in 1884 in a strapless black velvet dress, was described as a Creole in Deborah Davis's book *Strapless*, The portrait, known for its depiction of a red-haired woman with marblelike pale skin, caused a scandal at the time, supposedly, the art historians say, because wearing an off-the-shoulder strap was not a respectable way to appear. And unlike other images of the time, the bareness of the shoulders was without ornamentation or softness. Deborah Davis speculates that Madame Gautreau lost her place in society because of the representation in the painting, which her husband refused to buy. More interesting to me were the accounts of how some believe Madame Gautreau made her skin so white: with a trowel. It was noted that when she bathed in the ocean, the color was not diminished. One wonders if the knowledge of her Creole roots caused people to have uncommon interest in the color of her skin. I have always loved that painting for its beauty and grace. I'm sure I will never look at it again in the same way.

2

The Gift

A PASSING STORY

"When Waunetah Cotton and her younger brother, Ralph, applied for admission to a Los Angeles magnet school, their mother put down that they were black. Only one was accepted. Their mother was told that the magnet school had no more room for black students, but needed more white students. 'So she said, "Give the forms back and I'll change it." But they wouldn't let her,' said Cotton, 15. In the end, both enrolled in private schools.

"Cotton and her brother are Dutch with French and German ancestry on their mother's side, and African American, Navajo and Blackfoot on their father's side. Cotton, who has light skin, said that a Latino friend once asked her, 'What are you, white?' When she said 'no,' he said 'Yes you are.' Other people said: 'You're not black, you just have a year-round tan.' But she says she's not one or the other, but a mix of both, and more American than anything else."

(From "Not One or the Other: Teens Want Their
Multicultural Identities to be Recognized" by Jason
Sperber, LA Youth, *October 1991)*

In 1992, I gave my mother, Margaret Morris Taylor, an eightieth birthday present. The gift: her family. The family had separated themselves from her for seventy-six years. The present was the culmination of a promise I had made to my mother when I was twelve years old. Understanding that she had close relatives who were deliberately absent from her life, I believed it was my filial duty to fill the pages in her family album. Someday, I said, I will bring your family back to you. I will find out the reason for the separation and the long silence. More important, I will close the broken family circle. I will mend the shattered family wound and make us whole once again. All this from a girl in pigtails and bobby socks.

The ubiquitous Brownie cameras recorded the braids and the oxford fillers. The snapshots were pasted onto black pages. My mother cherished the sepia poses and Polaroid memories of the family she had created.

Years passed. Still trying out dreams, my husband and I moved to California. I found myself between opportunities. And I had some money from my last opportunity. I decided to use it to fulfill my coming-of-age pledge to my mother.

The forty-nine-dollar-find-anyone-in-the-country computer search engine had not yet come into easy access. Through a combination of time-consuming archival research and a private investigator, I was able to locate my mother's only living sibling, her eighty-eight-year-old only sister, Grace Morris Cramer.

Grace, who married and moved from Washington, D.C., to Delaware, to Buffalo, to Cleveland, and finally to Anaheim, California, was a widow whose only daughter, Patricia, had died. Patricia's three children, Jeffrey Scott, Lisa Scott, and Laura Scott Hoover, lived close by in neighboring suburbs. These grandchildren of Grace were the remains of her nuclear family. Everyone else she had previously claimed, including her beloved Irish grandmother, Margaret Maher, her unreliable and usually besotted father, Will Morris, and her favorite uncle, Edward Morris, was either dead or geographically remote. There was one exception: her sister, my mother, Margaret Morris Taylor, in Connecticut, whom Grace had not claimed over a span of three generations.

What had disunited Margaret from her family was the great divide, the Grand Canyon of separation: that peculiar thing we call "race" in America. One of my mother's paternal grandparents had been Irish, the other, what we would now call mixed race: His genetic heritage included African American, English, and Scott. Back then he was called a mulatto. Their children, including my mother's father, were fair skinned with straight hair. Or, in the parlance of that time and now, they "looked white."

They had come into the world classified as "mulattoes." In two subsequent censuses, census takers' subjective eyeballing evaluations and bureaucratic forms transformed them from "black" to "white." They were assumed to be white. They took the assumption one giant step farther. They "passed for white."

3

The Etiology of Passing

A PASSING STORY?

"How white are blacks? How black are whites? Because African-Americans and European-Americans have been in contact, sometimes intimate, since 1619, these questions are central to Americans' collective self-understanding. In recent years, genetic techniques for accurately determining the answers have finally become available.

"Molecular anthropologist Mark D. Shriver heads a group of nine population researchers at Penn State University who are going beyond the arbitrary 'one drop of blood' rule to answer these ancient questions about the family trees of the typical American 'black' and 'white.' They have examined DNA samples from 3,000 individuals in 25 locations around America, mostly self-identified African-Americans, looking for the gene markers that tend to differ between Europeans and Africans.

"Shriver pointed out that genetically tracking admixture is difficult because differences even between subraces, such as Scandinavian vs. West African, account for only about ten percent of human genetic variation. 'Thus we are all more alike than we are different,' he noted. . . .

"To Shriver, the most personally stunning of his findings involved one subject who reported himself to be completely white, yet whose genetic analysis showed that 22 percent of his relatively recent ancestors were African.

"'I had the result for two or three years before I even looked up the ID number of the person, whom we tested,' a bemused Shriver recounted. 'I looked at who it was and it was me! I checked myself and the rest of my relatives and tracked it through my family.'

"'I never considered there were any African people in my family,' remarked the 36-year-old Shriver, who looks like a typical white American. He has wavy brown hair and light skin that burns easily, but also tans darkly. His siblings look completely European, too. 'There's no real variation in my family. The admixture must have been pretty far back. It just so happens that we can detect it with the markers we have.

"'My mom especially stood out as being surprised, maybe because I told her it was coming through her father.' He credits his Catholic parents with providing him with a 'balanced, open, and egalitarian perspective about people. But, still, she doesn't believe it about her family!

"'The part of Pennsylvania where my mother's father came from is where the Underground Railroad ended,' Shriver observed, referring to the network that smuggled escaped slaves north to freedom. 'There are several towns right here in Southern Pennsylvania where there are very light-skinned African-American communities that are the remnant of the Underground Railroad.'

"His maternal grandfather moved from Pennsylvania to Iowa, then to California, leaving behind in the process most of his ties with his relatives. Shriver is considering trying to track down his maternal grandfather's relations in Pennsylvania."

*(From "White Prof Finds Out He's Not"
by Steve Sailer, UPI)*

Carla K. Bradshaw, a clinical psychologist and professor at the University of Washington, defined the passing process. "Passing is the word used to describe an attempt to achieve acceptability by claiming membership in some desired group while denying other racial elements in oneself thought to be undesirable. The concept of passing uses the imagery of camouflage, of concealing true identity of group membership and gaining false access. Concealment of 'true' identity is considered synonymous with compromised integrity and impostorship. . . . If an ideal world existed free from the psychology of dominance, where racial differences carried no stigma and racial purity was irrelevant, the concept of passing would have no meaning. In fact, passing of any kind loses meaning in the context of true egalitarianism."

Paul Spickard's *Mixed Blood*, a history of the subject, claims that passing has been occurring in America since the first contact between Africans and Europeans in 1608.

Up until the 1990s only sporadic artistic portrayals captured some of the issues of mixed-race people in the United States and their travails if they passed. One such was *Lost Boundaries*, a 1949 film based on "Document of a New Hampshire Family," a 1947 *Reader's Digest* account that also became a book. The true story was about a light-skinned family assumed to be white by the Keene, New Hampshire, community where they lived.

The chronicle tracks the real-life family of Dr. Albert C. Johnston, a black radiologist who graduated with honors from the University of Chicago's Rush Medical School and was offered and took over the practice of a beloved white physician. Both Johnston and his wife were fair skinned, and they had two fair-skinned children with whom they did not share the information about their black heritage.

Johnston's racial category was revealed after he applied for a commission in the navy, which investigated and uncovered his black heritage. The navy refused him the commission, the town found out, and his son left home to live in Harlem with black people.

Hollywood's happy endings had a local pastor become the white savior of the doctor and his family. The movie portrayed the U.S. government extending commissions to all men, regardless of race or color.

The Hollywood Reporter review of the film stated, "It is seldom written about, yet it is estimated that some 8,000,000 Negroes accomplish the deception of 'passing' as whites successfully." Where *The Reporter* garnered that figure is not evident in the review.

Atlanta, Georgia, city censor Christine Smith banned all screenings of *Lost Boundaries* because of its racial theme. According to *Variety,* Smith's edict was based on the city's ordinance that the censor was empowered to bar any picture that would "adversely affect the peace, morals and good order of the city." *Newsweek* in October 1949 reported that local censor Lloyd T. Binford had banned the film in Memphis because "In passing as white the Negro doctor in the film had slurred his own race by proving himself 'an impostor and a liar.'"

A federal lawsuit against the city of Atlanta ensued. Former Justice Samuel Rosenman, the prosecuting attorney in Atlanta, stated in November 1949 film trade papers that he hoped the suit would show deprivation of freedom of expression without due process of law, thereby testing the constitutionality of all censorship of motion pictures prior to public showing. According to the American Film Institute's Catalog of the 1940s, in opening arguments in the U.S. district court, Assistant City Attorney J. M. B. Bloodsworth, arguing the censor's side, alluded to a 1916 Supreme Court decision that films, as "spectacles," are not protected by the First Amendment. Rosenman responded, "Films are no longer a spectacle but a medium of information and opinion, as much or more than they are mere amusement. Our interests go beyond those of my client and of the motion picture industry. They should be of concern to all Americans interested in their freedom." The case went before the Fifth Circuit Court of Appeals, which upheld the Atlanta censor's decision. In October 1950, the U.S. Supreme Court refused to hear an appeal of the case.

In real life, Johnston continued to practice medicine in New Hampshire until the mid-1960s, when he moved to Hawaii with his wife. He died there in 1988. His son became a composer. Some of his songs were used for the movie about his family's life. The film itself won the award for best scenario for 1949 at the Cannes Film Festival.

Now, as America becomes more aware of its multiracial antecedents and genealogy has become the second-most-pursued hobby, the subject of passing has begun to resonate in popular culture. The popular television series *Law and Order* had an episode about a high-ranking "white" corporate executive who, at the height of his career, was newly identified as a black man. Although he himself was pale, he had had a dark-skinned child with his white wife. The assumption by others was that his wife had had an affair with a black man and the child was not her husband's. Such was not the case. The man had black genes, which he had kept secret.

Jennifer Beals played opposite Denzel Washington as a black woman passing for white in the film version of Walter Mosley's novel *Devil in a Blue Dress.* As I mentioned before, Philip Roth's book *The Human Stain,* about a classics professor passing for white in a prestigious university, became fodder for a movie starring Anthony Hopkins. Danzy Senna wrote the acclaimed novel *Caucasia* about a family separated by the color line. One sister passed for white while the other remained black. That was a little too close to home for me.

Although not exactly a tidal wave of material, these are significant forays into what for many white people is an unsettling or unbelievable topic. So unsettling, as journalist Brent Staples pointed out in a *New York Times* editorial, that American movie critics panned another well-known movie because they could not believe that a black man could successfully pass for white. It turned out that the movie had been based on the life of Walter White, a white-skinned, blue-eyed black man who was secretary of the National Association for the Advancement of Colored People in the 1930s, '40s, and early '50s. White passed for white without hindrance to investigate lynchings and other racially motivated crimes. He made his eyewitness reports to the NAACP to bolster the organization's antilynching efforts. And he used the incendiary material as the basis for two novels, *The Fire in Flint* (1924) and *Flight* (1926).

Why this incredulity still exists at the idea that black Americans could look like white Americans might be ascribed to hysterical blindness. My sense is that because of the deeply ingrained segregated lives Americans lead, except for the small numbers of people who make the effort to walk through the doors of other people's lives, there are scant insights into who the brown "others" are and how they live. It is taken for granted that "they" are different from "us" because of the color of their skin. The brightly burnished fact that we are all descendants of several hardy, resilient African groups that trekked out of Africa to the East, the North, and the West is a shiny coin that few whites want to keep in their change purses.

Our contemporary cultural differences create certitude among those who are white that as far as they know they themselves could be nothing but white. Anything else would be unthinkable. And, in the past, unacceptable. Not to mention the historical amnesia and/or denial about all the interracial couplings that have occurred since America's inception.

In *The History and Geography of Human Genes*, Stanford's Dr. L. L. Cavalli-Sforza reports that all ethnic groups hold an array of overlapping sets and subsets of mixed gene pools. He notes that modern Europeans (the ancestors of America's immigrants) have long been a mixed population whose genetic ancestry is 65 percent Asian and 35 percent African. There never has been any such thing as a "Caucasoid/Caucasian." Nor is there such a creature as a "pure" white or black American.

During hearings of the Senate Committee on Government Affairs on the Human Genome Diversity Project, Dr. Cavalli-Sforza and Dr. Mary-Claire King, a geneticist at the University of California at Berkeley, discussed the implications of their work. They called racism "an ancient scourge of humanity" and expressed the hope that further extensive study of world populations would help to "undercut conventional notions of race and underscore the common bonds between all humans."

4

Visible and Invisible

When I entered Wellesley College in 1955, a few weeks after fourteen-year-old Emmett Till was lynched in Money, Mississippi, I was one of three black women in my class. The international reaction to Till's death laid the foundation for the nascent civil rights movement.

One of the three black girls transferred to another school, leaving only two of us, the typical number of Negroes in each class of the Ivy League and Seven Sisters colleges at that time. Had she wanted to, the transferee could have passed for white. There is no record, of course, of black girls who had come to Wellesley earlier and crossed over the color line.

A PASSING STORY

Vassar "was the last of the Seven Sister colleges to knowingly admit African American students. The first known

Black student at Vassar was Anita Florence Hemmings, from Boston. She enrolled in 1893 and graduated in 1897. A scandal erupted throughout New England when it was discovered that Hemmings, who was light-skinned and passed for White, was actually African American. The event drew significant press coverage. One headline read: 'Negro Girl at Vassar: the handsomest girl there. Yale and Harvard Men among those who sought favor with the "brunette beauty."' Another article reported that 'Vassar girls are agitated over the report that one of the students in the senior class of '97 is of Negro parentage. She did not disclose the fact until just before graduation when statements made to Hemmings' roommate led to an investigation.' The article said that Hemmings had been noticed as being very bright as a young child, and that her early education had been financed by a wealthy White woman. Hemmings studied hard, passed the required examination, and entered Vassar. The article stated that 'Vassar is noted for its exclusiveness, and every official of the college refuses to say aught regarding this girl graduate.' Another source reported that the faculty was debating whether Hemmings should be denied her diploma. 'Never had a colored girl been a student at aristocratic Vassar, and professors were at a loss to foresee the effect upon the future if this one were allowed to be graduated.' In the end the faculty did consent to her graduation, reasoning that she was but a few days from commencement and, after this event, the girl would be gone and forgotten.

"While at Vassar, Hemmings was active in the Debate Society, College Glee Club, and the Contemporary Club Literary Organization. After graduating she worked at the Boston Public Library in the foreign cataloguing division.

She married a physician, and her daughter, Ellen Parker Love, graduated from Vassar in the class of 1927. Presumably Love passed for White as well, since her application stated that she was English and French. Hemmings's husband's race was unknown."

> *(From "The African American Female Elite: The Early History of African American Women in the Seven Sister Colleges, 1880–1960" by Linda M. Perkins,* Harvard Educational Review, *winter 1997)*

For a variety of reasons—economic, class, education, housing, and social acceptance—my mother's siblings, her father, one aunt, and one uncle decided, in the now antiquated phrase, to "pass for white." They tapped into America's yin and yang about skin color: an obsession and a denial of that obsession. Those who married and had children kept the secret of their heritage. I imagine that they worried that they might have little brown bundles of joy.

They left my mother and her little brother behind, to be cared for by a maternal cousin, a golden-skinned woman who could not pass. My mother's little brother died before he reached five. She was alone. For seventy-six years, none of my mother's family reached out to her again, until I began my search.

My mother became, in Walter White's words, "a visible Negro." White was fond of saying that for every visible Negro there was an invisible one: that is, one who was passing for white. When she was twenty-one, my mother married Julian Taylor, a young minister "the color of fresh-baked ginger cake." The reverend who walked debonairly into her life was from a prominent Washington, D.C., family, enormously proud of its hard-won accomplishments from Reconstruction onward.

From Washington they moved to Connecticut, where they had four children whose color ranged from eggnog to walnut. I was the third child born to their union. My father pastored a black church and marched through an activist life as a civil rights leader, an educator, and a planning commissioner for the mill town of Ansonia in the western hills of the state. Their life in Connecticut, from 1933 on, was socially schizophrenic, being both integrated and segregated. It was full and it was rich, providing me an unusually secure perch from which to view the world.

I had known, of course, since childhood of my missing family. I also knew that there were many black families like my own that had "lost" their kin. The phenomenon of passing was discussed whenever black people gathered together at weddings, funerals, christenings, and protest meetings. Invariably there were the stories of people showing up at funerals and the children asking, "Who are those white people?" Their parents would answer, "Those aren't white people; they're our relatives." To wit, just about every black family in America has a passing story.

Our loss and my mother's melancholy about it occupied its own special place in my psyche. It bothered me that I had a grandfather living "somewhere in Maryland" who had no interest in me or the fact that I was a straight-A student. It bothered me that I had first cousins "maybe in Cleveland, maybe in Buffalo" whom I could not know because my racial label would taint them. It bothered me that I had an aunt who had married a Harvard man, class of 1904, who had gone to live in South America because he could not get an engineering job as a black man in the United States. I just knew he had wondrous tales to tell a small-town niece like me.

It was fortunate for me that my father probably overcompensated by instilling in me and the rest of his family an unusually high sense of self-esteem and unlimited self-confidence.

Had we been allowed to see ourselves as unworthy, inferior creatures who deserved to be left on the "wrong" side of the color line, my life would have been entirely different. It is unlikely that I would have excelled in school, gone to a Seven Sisters college, attended Harvard University, and experienced some of the finest things that America can offer its most fortunate children.

All was well in my brown world, yet the family voids and the total absence of pictures or other images of my mother's family fueled my curiosity about my missing relatives. With all the self-righteous posturing adolescents can claim, I vowed at age twelve to right the wrongs in my family's life. I thought little of the consequences. Nor could I imagine them.

In 1992, on a crystalline blue September day, my husband and I drove my mother forty-five miles from Los Angeles to Anaheim to meet her older sister. I can re-create the scene over and over again, as if in slow motion. My mother crying, her faced deeply flushed as she reaches for her older sister in the doorway of a spotless trailer gleaming in the California morning sun.

Their two heads together, similarities notwithstanding, one labeled "white," the other "black" by a society relentless in its pigeonholing. They danced the "speech after long silence" dance. They bowed and curtsied to the rhythms of "How can I accommodate you in my life after seventy-six years of absence because we lived on different sides of the color line?" Minuet. Their fingers and their hearts met as they stroked a long-haired calico cat.

And afterward, at the end of that day, they parted as acknowledged sisters. There was no denying their striking physical similarities, their voice qualities, their gestures and mannerisms. There were still many gaps to fill, many aches to soothe, many questions to answer. But that would come. Together they had realized that they were more alike than different. Together they understood that America's history; not their father, was the villain in the piece. Together they realized that all who passed believed they were acting in the best interest of the family. Together they had toppled their personal pigmentocracy.

5

Passport to Privilege

In trying to understand why black people passed, I think it is important to lay out just what it is they were seeking. What besides the obvious did they believe they would gain?

After all, didn't America tell you that you had to get a good education—which often was not open to blacks? Didn't America tell you that you had to get a good job—which often was not available to blacks? Didn't America say you had to live in a nice neighborhood—which did not sell homes to blacks? Why, then, should they be penalized for their white skin? Why not take advantage of its unconscious privilege?

Some of the answers as to why people passed historically and still do in the present day may be found in a Rosetta stone list of what it means to be the recipient of white privilege. Peggy McIntosh formulated this astonishing list in a groundbreaking working paper titled "White Privilege: Unpacking the Invisible Knapsack" in 1988 for the Wellesley College Center for Research on Women. When I came across her piece, I felt that I had not only pierced some type of racial veil, but that I had also been given the keys to the kingdom of whiteness.

She wrote, "I think whites are carefully taught not to recognize white privilege as males are taught not to recognize male privilege. As a white person, I realized I had been taught about racism as something which puts others at a disadvantage, but had been taught not to see one of its corollary aspects, white privilege which puts me at an advantage. . . . I have come to see white privilege as an invisible package of unearned assets which I can count on cashing in each day, but about which I was 'meant' to remain oblivious. White privilege is like an invisible weightless knapsack of special provisions, assurances, tools, maps, guides, codebooks, passports, visas, clothes, compass, emergency gear and blank checks.

"Then I remembered the frequent charges from women of color that white women whom they encounter are oppressive. I began to understand why we are justly seen as oppressive, even when we don't see ourselves that way. At the very least, obliviousness of one's privileged state can make a person or group irritating to be with. I began to count the ways in which I enjoy unearned skin privilege and have been conditioned into oblivion about its existence, unable to see that it put me 'ahead' in any way, or put my people ahead, over-rewarding us and yet also paradoxically damaging us, or that it could or should be changed."

McIntosh goes on to say, "My schooling gave me no training in seeing myself as an oppressor, as an unfairly advantaged person, or as a participant in a damaged culture. I was taught to see myself as an individual whose moral state depended on her individual moral will. At school, we were not taught about slavery in any depth; we were not taught to see slaveholders as damaged people. Slaves were seen as the only group at risk of being dehumanized. My schooling followed the pattern . . . [that] whites are taught to think of their lives as morally neutral, normative and average, and also ideal, so that when we work to benefit others, this is seen as work which will allow 'them' to be more like 'us.'"

McIntosh reported, "I have decided to work on myself at least by identifying some of the daily effects of white privilege in my life. It is crude work, at this stage, but I will give here a list of special circumstances and conditions I experience which I did not earn but which I have been made to feel are mine by birth, by citizenship, and by virtue of being a conscientious law abiding 'normal' person of good will. I have chosen those conditions which I think in my case attach somewhat more to skin-color privilege than to class, religion, ethnic status, or geographical location, though of course all these other factors are intricately intertwined. As far as I can see, my Afro-American coworkers, friends, and acquaintances with whom I come into daily or frequent contact in this particular time, place and line of work cannot count on most of these conditions."

Peggy McIntosh's White Privilege List

"1. I can if I wish arrange to be in the company of people of my race most of the time.

"2. I can avoid spending time with people whom I was trained to mistrust and who have learned to mistrust my kind and me.

"3. If I should need to move, I can be pretty sure of renting or purchasing housing in an area which I can afford and in which I would want to live.

"4. I can be pretty sure that my neighbors in such a location will be neutral or pleasant to me.

"5. I can go shopping almost most of the time, pretty well assured that I will not be followed or harassed.

"6. I can turn on the television or open to the front page of the paper and see people of my race widely represented.

"7. When I am told about our national heritage or about 'civilization,' I am shown that people of my color made it what it is.

"8. I can be sure that my children will be given curricular materials that testify to the existence of their race.

"9. If I want to, I can be pretty sure of finding a publisher for this piece on white privilege.

"10. I can be pretty sure of having my voice heard in a group in which I am the only member of my race.

"11. I can be casual about whether or not to listen to another woman's voice in a group in which she is the only member of her race.

"12. I can go into a music shop and count on finding the music of my race represented, into a supermarket and find the staple foods which fit with my cultural traditions, into a hairdresser's shop and find someone who can cut my hair.

"13. Whether I use checks, credit cards, or cash, I can count on my skin color not to work against the appearance of financial responsibility.

"14. I can arrange to protect my children most of the time from people who might not like them.

"15. I do not have to educate my children to be aware of systemic racism for their own daily physical protection.

"16. I can be pretty sure that my children's teachers and employers will tolerate them if they fit school and workplace norms; my chief worries about them do not concern others' attitudes toward their race.

"17. I can talk with my mouth full and not have people put this down to my color.

"18. I can swear, or dress in second hand clothes, or not answer letters, without having people attribute these choices to the bad morals, the poverty, or the illiteracy of my race.

"19. I can speak in public to a powerful male group without putting my race on trial.

"20. I can do well in a challenging situation without being called a credit to my race.

"21. I am never asked to speak for all the people of my racial group.

"22. I can remain oblivious of the language and customs of persons of color who constitute the world's majority without feeling in my culture any penalty for such oblivion.

"23. I can criticize our government and talk about how much I fear its policies and behavior without being seen as a cultural outsider.

"24. I can be pretty sure that if I talk to 'the person in charge' I will be facing a person of my race.

"25. If a traffic cop pulls me over or if the IRS audits my tax return, I can be sure I haven't been singled out because of my race.

"26. I can easily buy posters, post-cards, picture books, greeting cards, dolls, toys and children's magazines featuring people of my race.

"27. I can go home from most meetings or organizations I belong to feeling somewhat tied in, rather than isolated, out-of-place, outnumbered, unheard, held at a distance, or feared.

"28. I can be pretty sure that an argument with a colleague of another race is more likely to jeopardize her chances for advancement than to jeopardize mine.

"29. I can be pretty sure that if I argue for the promotion of a person of another race, or a program centering on race, this is not likely to cost me heavily within my present setting, even if my colleagues disagree with me.

"30. If I declare there is a racial issue at hand, or there isn't a racial issue at hand, my race will lend me more credibility for either position than a person of color will have.

"31. I can choose to ignore developments in minority writing and minority activist programs, or disparage them, or learn from them, but in any case, I can find ways to be more or less protected from negative consequences of any of these choices.

"32. My culture gives me little fear about ignoring the perspectives and powers of people of other races.

"33. I am not made acutely aware that my shape, bearing, or body odor will be taken as a reflection of my race.

"34. I can worry about racism without being seen as self-interested or self-seeking.

"35. I can take a job with an affirmative action employer without having my co-workers on the job suspect that I got it because of my race.

"36. If my day, week, or year is going badly, I need not ask of each negative episode or situation whether it has racial overtones.

"37. I can be pretty sure of finding people who would be willing to talk with me and advise me about my next steps, professionally.

"38. I can think over many options, social, political, imaginative or professional, without asking whether a person of my race would be accepted or allowed to do what I want to do.

"39. I can be late to a meeting without having the lateness reflect on my race.

"40. I can choose public accommodations without fearing that people of my race cannot get in or will be mistreated in the places I have chosen.

"41. I can be sure that if I need legal or medical help, my race will not work against me.

"42. I can arrange my activities so that I will never have to experience feelings of rejection owing to my race.

"43. If I have low credibility as a leader, I can be sure that my race is not the problem.

"44. I can easily find academic courses and institutions which give attention only to people of my race.

"45. I can expect figurative language and imagery in all of the arts to testify to experiences of my race.

"46. I can choose blemish cover or bandages in 'flesh' color and have them more or less match my skin."

McIntosh admitted, "I repeatedly forgot each of the realizations on this list until I wrote it down. For me, white privilege has turned out to be an elusive and fugitive subject. The pressure to avoid it is great, for in facing it I must give up the myth of meritocracy. If these things are true, this is not such a free country; one's life is not what one makes it; many doors open for certain people through no virtues of their own. These perceptions mean also that my moral condition is not what I had been led to believe. The appearance of being a good citizen rather than a troublemaker comes in large part from having all sorts of doors open automatically because of my color. . . .

"In unpacking this invisible knapsack of white privilege, I have listed conditions of daily experience which I once took for granted, as neutral, normal, and universally available to everybody, just as I once thought of a male-focused curriculum as the neutral or accurate account which can speak for all. Nor did I think of any of these perquisites as bad for the holder. I now think that we need a more finely differentiated taxonomy of privilege, for some of these varieties are not only what one would want for everyone in a just society, and others give license to be ignorant, oblivious, arrogant and destructive. . . ."

McIntosh continues, "In this potpourri of examples, some privileges make me feel at home in the world. Others allow me to escape penalties or dangers which others suffer. Through some, I escape fear, anxiety, or a sense of not being welcome or not being real. Some keep me from having to hide, to be in disguise, to feel sick or crazy, to negotiate each transaction from the position of being an outsider, or within my group, a person who is suspected of having too close links with a dominant culture. Most keep me from having to be angry.

"I see a pattern running through the matrix of white privilege, a pattern of assumptions which were passed on to me as a white person. There was one main piece of cultural turf; it was my own turf, and I was among those who could control the turf. I could measure up to the cultural standards and take advantage of the many options I saw around me to make what the culture would call a success of my life. *My skin color was an asset for any move I was educated to want to make.* I could think of myself as 'belonging' in major ways, and of making social systems work for me. I could freely disparage, fear, neglect, or be oblivious to anything outside of the dominant cultural forms. Being of the main culture, I could also criticize it fairly freely. My life was reflected back to me frequently enough so that I felt, with regard to my race, if not to my sex, like one of the real people."

McIntosh opined, "Whether through the curriculum or in the newspaper, the television, the economic system, or the general look of people in the streets, we received daily signals and indications that my people counted, and that others *either didn't exist or must be trying, not very successfully, to be like people of my race.* We were given cultural permission not to hear voices of people of other races, or a tepid cultural tolerance for hearing or acting on such voices. I was also raised not to suffer seriously from anything which darker-skinned people might say about my group, 'protected' though perhaps I should more accurately say *prohibited through* the habits of my economic class and social group, from living in racially mixed groups or being reflective about interactions between people of differing races."

McIntosh concluded, "In proportion as my racial group was being made confident, comfortable, and oblivious, other groups were likely being made inconfident, uncomfortable, and alienated. Whiteness protected me from many kinds of hostility, distress and violence, which I was being subtly trained to visit in turn upon people of color. . . . Such privilege simply *confers dominance,* gives permission to control, because of one's race or sex. The kind of privilege which gives license to some people to be, at best, thoughtless, and at worst, murderous should not continue to be referred to as a desirable attribute. Such 'privilege' may be widely desired without being in any way beneficial to the whole society. . . . In some groups, those dominated have actually become strong through not having all of these unearned advantages, and this gives them a great deal to teach the others. Members of so-called privileged groups can seem foolish, ridiculous, infantile or dangerous by contrast. . . . In my class and place, I did not see myself as racist because I was taught to recognize racism only in individual acts of meanness by members of my group, never in invisible systems conferring unsought racial dominance on my group from birth. . . . A 'white' skin in the United States opens many doors for whites whether or not we approve of the way dominance has been conferred on us. . . . To redesign social systems we need first to acknowledge their colossal unseen dimensions. The silences and denials surrounding privilege are the key political tool here. They keep the thinking about equality or equity incomplete, protecting unearned advantage and conferred dominance by making these taboo subjects. . . .

"It seems to me that obliviousness about white advantage, like obliviousness about male advantage, is kept strongly inculturated in the United States so as to maintain the myth of meritocracy, the myth that democratic choice is equally available to all. Keeping most people unaware that freedom of confident action is there for just a small number of people props up those in power, and serves to keep power in the hands of the same groups that have most of it already."

I happened onto Peggy McIntosh's paper by accident the same year it was written. I was overwhelmed with the power of her confessional. I had neither seen, heard, nor read anything like it in my professional or personal life. It did call to mind the work of Lillian Smith, author of the 1949 book *Killers of the Dream*, which I had read breathlessly and bug-eyed as a teenager. Smith wrote about what it felt like to be a Southern white woman who did not like or agree with the privileges she had at the expense of colored people. I wondered when I read her book why so few other whites had written about their dissatisfaction with the way things were between the races.

I told the story of the search for and recovery of my family in *The Sweeter the Juice,* which I started not as a book but as a birthday manuscript for my mother. The drama, pathos, and universality of the story called out for sharing. The response to the story has been overwhelming and, in the words of Duke Ellington, "beyond category." What follows is a continuation of my family's journey around, through, and beyond America's color line.

6

A Place Beyond Loss

A PASSING STORY

In South Africa in the 1960s, a little girl named Sandra Laing "wished she could wiggle out of her skin and shed her color like the molting snakes that rustled through the green fields. . . . She was the daughter of white Afrikaners who proudly supported the government's brutal system of apartheid and racial segregation."

Sandra's skin was honey brown. Her birth certificate said white, but "she was a brown child living in a white world." Her parents both had white skin. She was not adopted, and tests showed that both her parents were her biological parents. There were whispers that African blood flowed through their veins.

When Sandra was fifteen, her white classmates complained about her color. She was expelled from her all-white school and disowned by her parents and brothers. The government reclassified her as black. She became separated from her mother and brothers for twenty-seven years, not seeing her mother again until the mother was seventy-nine and living in a nursing home.

Now Sandra lives a modest, circumscribed life in a black township, often too destitute to afford the seventy-two cents it costs to make a ten-minute phone call to her mother. Once her brothers wrote to her, offering to pay her off if she would leave them and her mother alone. Explaining his separation from his sister, her brother said, "I've got my wife and kids to think of. You understand? I have to keep them safe."

The *Times* said, "The siblings will probably never know whether their family had a black ancestor somewhere." What reporters and others don't seem to get is that if you have an ancestor of color, chances are that someone in the family will have a baby of color.

> (From *"Apartheid Still Burdens a Girl Who Didn't Fit"*
> *by Rachel L. Swarns*, The New York Times,
> *June 10, 2000*)

How do we become who we are? The formation of the self is probably a never-ending process beginning in the womb and ending in the casket. The changeling we call the self is a repository of parenting, sibling and family experiences, education, image absorption, and simply moving through life. We look in the mirror every day, and the face that peers back is never quite the same. In a similar, nonquantifiable process, our invisible persona shifts—subtly, perhaps, or even substantially—depending on our understanding and acceptance of the day's events.

Lately, I have been thinking a great deal about the question of my self—whether it has changed substantially, and if so how much, as a result of the dramatic developments in my family's life. After many long years and through a concerted research effort, I found a part of my family that had virtually disappeared more than seventy-six years ago. Since the reunification occurred, I have been trying to sort out what impact the closing of the family circle has had on me and those closest to me.

Before a recent Thanksgiving holiday, I was polishing some crystal glasses, which my maiden godmother had given me when I was sixteen. As the sun gleamed through a thin, gold-rimmed water glass (to be used only at lunch and *never* at dinner, I was carefully instructed), I thought of my great-uncle Eddie Scott. He was the brother of my mother's mother, Rose Scott. Now, I must admit that looking for spots on drinking glasses and polishing crystal is something I reluctantly tend to three times a year: Thanksgiving, Christmas, and Easter—and just possibly for a special birthday dinner party. Why should this content-free, unwelcome activity bring to mind a long-dead uncle whom I had only heard about and never knew?

For more than a quarter of a century, Edward Scott was the valet and majordomo for a rich and socially prominent family, the Riggses of Washington, D.C. Some said he was the epitome of a gentleman's gentleman. I could imagine him standing in the large white butler's pantry imperiously inspecting the glasses before sumptuous dinner parties for Washington's elite, during the era before the First World War and on into the late '20s. Since he died when my mother was a teenager and before I was born, I never met him. I have a much-cherished picture of him, though. For a long time, this was the only photograph my mother had of any of her family members.

Eddie was not quite white. He was a fair-skinned man with gray eyes and straight hair. To the untrained eye he probably appeared to be a prosperous upper-class white gentleman. Although he was indeed "white" on his job, where he supervised an Irish staff—with one other undetected exception, my godmother, Rosa—he was black on the weekends and whenever else he needed to be for his family. Sociologists call the kind of passing Eddie and Rosa participated in "discontinuous passing," because those who assume different racial identities do so only part-time, usually for economic reasons.

Why would anyone pass to be in the servant class? At that time in Washington, many of the wealthy hired only white servants, often immigrants. For those without schooling, working in-service was often the best opportunity to come their way. It was also a way to observe the mores and manners of the cultured and the truly genteel.

But such passing was not without costs. Eddie's employers did not know he was black until he dropped dead unexpectedly and unceremoniously on a Washington street. When one of the employer's family accompanied the chauffeur to notify and pick up Eddie's niece, my mother, the family member was shocked to learn that she lived in a black neighborhood. And later, that same employer arranged that the bulk of Eddie's estate should be shared and controlled by his nephews and nieces who lived as white in other towns.

They—my mother's brothers and one sister, that is—passed continuously. They had cut off all ties with my mother, their heritage, and their assigned race of origin. Like thousands of other light-skinned black Americans, they took the journey through the American looking glass of race and came out on the other side. The pier glass did not betray them.

It is true that in the early 1900s, life was complex and often horrendously difficult for the descendants of slaves. Recessions came and went, creating limited employment opportunities.

Waves of immigrants vied for whatever security their new country could give them. Those jobs that did exist, for the most part, went to whites. Jim Crow laws, separating the races, were put into place. Lynchings were commonplace and their numbers were growing.

I have been told that these were some of the reasons that people "passed for white." Of course, there were many black people of light color who did not pass, who survived, and some of whom achieved. But that was not what my mother's family chose to do. Life had been too hard for them, I guess. For them, the future could not be bright unless it was white. For them, white skin meant civil treatment. For them, whiteness meant exploring in an unfettered way and growing with the ever-expanding America. For them, white skin meant unlimited opportunities. Or so they thought.

And so those old enough in my mother's family to understand made a covenant to leave behind rage and anger and sanction and second-class citizenship. They would leave behind definitions of themselves as animals, beasts, simpletons, and primitive souls. They would leave behind the stereotypes that they smelled and had no morals. They would leave behind the notions that they were lazy, bug-eyed, and oversexed.

By the simple act of moving to another place, they would happily take up the white man's burden. They would in fact become the white man. They acted on the complexly simple infinitive "to be," and in fact they "became," they "were," and their descendants still "are" "white."

There was never any question in my mind that I was a colored girl. I'd received this message loud and clear from both of my parents. My mother made it clear in her choice of husband, a proud, dark-skinned minister. Julian was one of five sons of another proud, dark-skinned minister who had completed college in the 1890s, a rare feat for Americans of any color at that time. My grandfather had also been a history teacher and suffused his household with black history long before it became a curriculum item.

Thus in my father's house there were books, journals, stories, magazine articles, and newspaper columns about American blacks from their earliest introduction to this country. Underscoring our accessibility to information about the black experience was the position held by one of my father's brothers, editor of *The Pittsburgh Courier,* one of America's most influential black newspapers. In addition, my grandfather passed along the history of his own life in letters, sermons, newspaper articles, and photographs. These became central in the mantra of my life, very much a colored life.

I remember my family as a large group of lively people, beautifully brown in all of its permutations. My father seemed to be the lightning rod of the family, keeping in touch with his brothers by mail, phone, and visits. He emphasized the importance of family integrity, family achievement, and family closeness. He made certain that his children kept in touch with their aunts and uncles and cousins as well.

It was the photographs of my father's family that as a child impressed me the most. Faces, beautiful brown faces, bearing witness to a legacy of strength and dignity. I had no similar pictures of my mother's family.

Buttressing the pictures and the written word was the life we lived. Although we experienced what was, on the surface at least, a mostly racially integrated small-town life, my identity was forged in the crucible of the black Baptist church, which my father pastored for the first forty-two years of my life. The majority of his parishioners had migrated from towns in the

Carolinas with names like Society Hill and Pinetops. Leaving behind dream-crushing lives as sharecroppers in the cotton and tobacco fields of the South, they came to the Connecticut mill town in which we lived. From them I would intimately learn about, deeply appreciate, and sincerely respect the mores and folkways of poor black people from the South.

I grew up indulged and somewhat privileged. We lived in lovely homes, traveled to many parts of the country, wore beautiful clothes, and knew that our black family was special. My father sent my sisters and me to fine schools without the benefit of major scholarships or affirmative action.

We married exceptional men, parented children who went to college and stayed out of trouble, and lived interesting lives.

There were people and situations, of course, that tested our values, challenged our freedom, and resented our right to thrive because we were black. But the strength of character our parents endowed us with caused us to continually challenge racial barriers, reject racial constraints, and push for racial equality. We seemed to be whole.

Although I never met my father's father, because he died the year I was born, abundant documentation of his life, his loves, and his career surrounded me. Because he was a public figure—he founded a large Baptist church in Washington, D.C.—I still meet people who can share anecdotes about him. Although he was dead, his persona was very much present in my life. And I was so proud of him.

And so the heritage that I knew was a source of strength for me. But there was the other side. The unfilled pages of the ledger. The family tree with truncated limbs. The blank leaves in the scrapbook reserved for but not taken by my mother's family.

As far as I was concerned, although I had six cousins, I did not have enough in my peer group. There was really only one near my age, and she lived in North Carolina. Thus I would fantasize about my mother's siblings' children. I chose to believe that I had these girl cousins out there with whom I would have been great friends. Had they been closer, I thought, we would have gone to the movies, camp, shopping, and maybe even college together. I wondered about them often. I knew they existed, but in what configuration of age, size, and shape I had no idea. A simple walk down a shaded street on a summer afternoon with one of my absent cousins was a recurring childhood fantasy for me.

When I was a little girl, my mother would take me and my siblings to visit my godmother, Rosa, the first maid at the mansion where Uncle Eddie had become her fiancé. Eddie was long gone by the time we came to enjoy "his" house. The annual visit was always in the close summer heat of August and always when the rest of the staff was in Bar Harbor, Maine, at their summer workplace. Rosa was left in charge and alone.

After inspecting the mammoth kitchen and butler's pantry, then exercising our imaginations about what was under the shrouded white shapes in the great downstairs rooms, we would have lunch and lemonade exquisitely served on the best china, with the finest silver and the thinnest crystal, on a flagstone terrace. I could not leave until I had my annual swing in what seemed to be a replica of someone's idea of a secret garden, profuse and redolent with every kind of summer blossom imaginable. It must be heaven to be rich, I thought. I was too young to put skin color into that equation.

In the quiet, sleepy afternoon on the grounds of the mansion, no other souls were in sight. Although my mother was light and could be mistaken for white, Rosa could not risk being caught with a bunch of tanned children, even if they were her family members and extraordinarily well bred and presentable. I would not know this until later, though.

After Eddie died, Rosa never married, nor did she have children. She worked at the mansion until she retired, well into her eighties. She lived a quiet, private, and I think lonely life in her own elegant brownstone in Washington, a home that, in its tone and furnishings, reflected her employer's understated, expensive taste. Later in life I wondered if she did not marry because she could not find someone like Eddie who had lived two lives in two worlds, someone who could understand her perspective.

Another object of my childhood fantasy caused by the cleft in my family was the life of my great-aunt Ruth and great-uncle John in Brazil. It was through John's letters to his Harvard alumni magazine that I learned of his interest in butterflies, reading, travel, and solitude.

With more than a pang of regret, I thought back to those times when I was a teenager oozing romantic thoughts from every pore, reading everything in sight, listening to fervent ballads late at night. There I was, yearning to know about the world, not knowing I had this brilliant, quirky, gentle uncle out there, chasing exotic winged creatures and taking trips through the Brazilian rain forests.

For some reason I imagined that if I had known them, my great-aunt Ruth would have been less accessible to me than her husband. In my research I recovered photos of her that reflected an extremely tall, glamorous figure with a Modigliani neck and a Mona Lisa smile. How far away her upper-class white life in São Paulo seemed from my growing-up years in a Connecticut factory town. I wonder at what intersection Ruth and I would have connected. It might have been through her clothes, since my mother dressed well and I was a fashion-conscious teenager. Ruth's inner life remains a pale, shimmering mystery to me captured in an oil painting of her in an elegant fur coat, sometime around 1917.

It is natural that I should wonder a lot about my mother's father, Will Morris. He died when I was a junior in college, the same year I met the man who would be my husband. Yet I never knew Will. While I was growing up in Connecticut, he was living not too far away as a white man in a little hamlet on Maryland's Eastern Shore, an area that was said to be rich in prejudices against black people. His absence had inflicted a deep wound on my mother, some of the poison of which seeped into me.

As I was putting together the puzzle of my mother's life, she and I found out together that her father had been an alcoholic with erratic work habits. Learning that he had been an irresponsible drifter who had virtually abandoned all of his family strangely enough offered some measure of peace to my mother. At least she had not been singled out, as she had thought all those years. They say the gene for alcoholism is both inherited and passed on. I have never been a drinker, and I wonder if there is some unconscious force of rejection of my grandfather at work in this.

In the last few years, I have seen numerous pictures of my grandfather, from his adolescence on. He was a beautiful child who became a handsome man. But at some point, probably because of alcohol and hard times, his looks broke. In his last pictures, taken in his eighties, his face reflected years of pain and difficulty. Would his life have been better as a black man? Probably not. After all, during his teens he had been called a "white nigger." In those years, his whiteness would have made his blackness a source of unease for both groups. There would never have been a day when he would not have had to take some kind of blackness test.

I have learned to feel sorry for Will Morris. Sorry that I did not know him. Sorry that he left my mother and the rest of his family. Sorry that he probably had little inner peace. Sorry that society could not just let him be.

As a child, it was difficult for me to understand how someone could abandon my good, kind, beautiful mother. Although "passing" was explained to me, I could not at first fathom how my relatives could be white while we were colored. In my world then, where two and two added up to four, black on one side of my family and white on the other did not come out an even sum. Somehow white always had more points. It made no sense.

It was perfectly natural that I wanted to know what it was like to pass. I wanted to *see* these people with whom I shared a gene pool. I wanted to *see* if they looked like me. Did they eat fish on Fridays? Were they as smart as we were? And why had they left my mother behind? Why had they made her so sad? I wanted to know. But more important, I wanted to *see*.

I would finally get my wish. I *saw*. Although the trip from Los Angeles to Anaheim, where my mother's sister lived, was short in mileage, it was long in history and emotion. It was probably my journey of a lifetime.

What I saw surprised me. My aunt Grace was a tiny woman, almost an exact replica of my mother. I had never seen anyone look like my mother before. Common sense should have told me that she would look like my mother. But the emotional knowledge that she had passed for white caused me to presume she would look like someone else. I, a child of America's anxiety about authenticity, America's paranoia about purity, America's preoccupation with differences, just *knew* she would somehow be "different."

Grace smiled at me, a sweet, inquisitive, almost tentative smile. With dizzying swiftness I thought of all the years I had waited to see that smile, hoping it would be kind but fearing that it might not. I crossed her threshold in the present but went back into the past. Would I, could I, make up for any of the time, the love, the emotional resonance lost? Would Grace "recognize" me? Could she do that without giving up all or part of the persona that she had claimed for the last seventy-six years? Would I catch a glimpse of the little girl of twelve who had been separated from her sister so long ago?

Our bridging began in a way that was fragile, tentative, and circumspect. I could not blurt out too quickly the really deep, troubling questions about the past, for fear of withdrawal and anxiety and guilt—all of which were sure to be present, anyway. Talking about our lives as we were living them in the present provided a comfort zone for both of us.

One of Grace's favorite subjects was her poetically handsome uncle Edward, her father's brother. He and his wife, Minette, had fled to Buffalo and lived among the white burghers. They had been very good to Grace and in fact had left her part of their estate, which she said she had never collected.

Grace loved Edward. I got the feeling that he had spoiled her like no one else of his generation ever had. She reported that he was as kind as he was handsome. His greatest achievement was working on the Peace Bridge, a structure that spanned the Niagara River from Buffalo to Fort Erie. His name is engraved on a plaque along with many other artisans who erected the connector. He was proudest of the fact that another Edward, the Prince of Wales, along with his brother Prince George, had borne witness to his work, drawing mammoth publicity as "the royals" officiated at the ceremonies dedicating the span to the citizens of both towns.

Later, I found a picture of my great-uncle Edward from that period. He was carrying a miniature schnauzer and wearing a tweed suit that might have been tailored by the king's tailor. I was struck by how much he looked like a more manly version of the Duke of Windsor.

Edward died of throat cancer when I was in grammar school. Just as my mother had no knowledge of his life, she was not notified of his death. Sometimes I think of my girlhood self in pigtails and a freshly starched pinafore. How I would have loved listening to this tall, handsome man tell stories about the dangers and excitement of building a bridge for modern America and how it felt to be in close proximity to a once and future king of England. What wonderful stuff that would have made for my prepubescent fantasies.

Perhaps for me the two most stunningly sad family revelations were that my mother's last surviving brother, Bill, had died in 1980 and that Grace's only child, Patricia, my cousin who would have been my contemporary, had died prematurely in 1982. So close in time and yet a lifetime away.

In 1980 my husband, daughters, and I had just returned to Connecticut from living in the Virgin Islands. We had been in St. Thomas for eight years. During that time, both my uncle Bill and my cousin Patricia contracted cancer. How difficult for the families. How regretful that we could not be among those who would comfort and support them. Although we had been in the islands, we might as well have been on a different planet in terms of the universe of our white family.

Long after the fact I learned that Patricia had been studious and enjoyed reading as much as I did. I would know her later only through the gallery of pictures that her doting mother had kept. There she was as a preteen, wearing sausage curls as I had worn (only hers were straighter). But that cherubic image did not begin to approach the landscape I wanted to detail. It was not nearly enough. From her own words, I wanted to know the timbre of her voice, the colors she preferred, the classes she liked, the sports she enjoyed, and the boys she turned down.

There is a saving grace. I now know Pat's three children, and in them, I see some aspects of her. The feeling that I would like to have known *her* has not left me.

When I see all the pictures of my mother's brother Bill, I wonder how somebody could not have known or suspected he had black heritage. Even one of his daughters said that except for his light coloring, he looked like many black men she had seen. As a "white" supervisor of black crews working in a steel factory in Cleveland, Bill had the respect of his men. I wonder now if some of those black men, accustomed to a spectrum of color in their race, understood or believed that their boss was "passing."

I wish I could have asked Bill about those difficult years just before and after he left Washington. What regrets, if any, did he have in leaving his black life behind? How fearful had he been of being "found out"? Was he concerned that his children might "look black"? Did he ever think of my mother? Did he care that he had three little tan nieces and a nephew who looked like his father?

My mother had another brother named Sumner whom she remembered better than Bill, because he remained in Washington a little longer. He worked as a white vendor in the open-air O Street Market. A guardian took my mother to see Sumner there several times, but he did not acknowledge her. He moved to Landover, Maryland. My mother never saw or heard from him again, although she once set out to make contact.

As I was on a chartered bus heading for the mammoth arena in Landover and the Inaugural Gala in honor of President Clinton, I thought about my mother's effort to reach out to Sumner as she had related it to me many times over the years. Landover had become quite an imaginary location for me, a place occupied by only one citizen, my mother's missing brother.

One picture of Sumner has come to light. He is in a military uniform of the First World War, sitting in the center of a group

of other white men. His position suggests that he was somewhat of a leader. His looks would certainly have allowed for
that, handsome strong features and clear light eyes. He is smiling as if he is hugely self-satisfied. As if he would continue to
lead those conquering heroes on whatever expedition they
might be assigned. I wonder now what those men would have
thought, how they would have reacted, if they had known that
the man in their midst was a pretender, that he was indeed what
they would have considered a Negro.

Had I seen that picture as a young girl, I would have been
enormously intrigued. I would have coupled that photo with
one in my father's photo album: one of my paternal uncles in
leather boots, uniform, and an officer's cap, astride a horse.
Never mind that that uncle was of a considerably darker hue
and serving in an all-Negro unit in the Second World War. To
me, they were both soldiers.

And so as the bus rumbled toward Landover in the soft gray
light of early evening, I was filled with an odd feeling, a yearning,
perhaps. Would my mother's life have been different then had she
made contact with Sumner? Although she had his address and
directions to where he lived, she could not take the final steps of
that journey. She explains now that she was too afraid of rejection, denial, and humiliation. She let the situation remain as it was
but excoriated herself thereafter for her timidity.

I too wonder if my mother did the right thing. She was in
her thirties, then, with four young children and a busy husband. She clearly had her own life, but the wound from what
she believed was her family's rejection still festered. It was in
the '40s, and rural Landover was in racist country. Sumner had
married a white wife and was living on a farm, raising white
chickens. Because I have no idea of the nature of Sumner's

character, there is no way to know how that scene would have played itself out had my mother driven up his driveway. To this day, I wonder and imagine.

Finding the descendants of my mother's siblings has been an unexpectedly joyful experience. They are alive and well, thriving in towns like Red Wing, Minnesota; Chesterland, Ohio; Denver, Colorado; San Francisco, California; and Brea, California. We have compared notes on the story of our family as it had been told to us and on the history as it has been reconstructed. In our exchanges we have all learned how history can be skillfully crafted to fit the historian's needs or preferred version of the truth. We understand well the meaning of *Rashomon.*

My cousins and their children have not hidden the newly acquired facts of their heritage from their white friends and home communities. One invited me to the college where she teaches to be a speaker in the institution's cultural diversity series. Another invited me to her engagement party in Orange County, California, and her wedding in Red Wing, Minnesota. At the California party she proudly introduced me, my husband, and my mother to all of her guests, many of whom had read the book written about her family. She embraced the fact of her black heritage with gusto and curiosity in equal measure. And another "new" cousin decided to celebrate Kwanzaa in her home, as a way to begin to incorporate another culture into her roots.

What has been the downside for them, if any, is their story to tell. One of them did tell me that she had never considered herself racist; had not, in fact, thought much about black people. Nor had she considered what a totally white world she inhabited. She was used to hearing racial slurs but had never taken them to heart, she said. Now she does. In fact, she has started to keep a journal of racial remarks that come her way during the day.

The number of people who have approached me across the

country and begun the conversation with almost the identical line, "I had a black grandparent," has been a revelation. It is clear that in their sharing this information, they are telling me that they consider themselves white but that they "understand" what happened in my family.

It occurred to me that many of them did not or do not realize that blacks and many white people without similar ancestry—as far as they know—would consider the confessors black because of the fabled "one drop" rule. Indeed, until 1987, when all "one drop" laws were nullified or rescinded except in Louisiana, those who were determined to uphold racial dividing lines would have declared these grandchildren who had one progenitor with black heritage, black.

Perhaps the best line shared with me was "We were colored once, but it stopped with Granddaddy," uttered with the greatest sincerity by a blue-eyed, red-haired, pale woman of a certain age in a mall in Southern California. I am not sure whether this recognition of genes but rejection of racial assignment was a denial of the past or an acceptance of the future.

7

Creating a New Vocabulary

A PASSING STORY

Not long ago, I spoke at a country club to a women's group in a wealthy suburb of San Diego. When I looked out over a sea of faces, I noticed that there was not one person of color. Not unusual, I suppose, for that part of Southern California.

When I had concluded my presentation and was sitting at a table signing books, a pretty white-haired woman in her sixties leaned over the table and said, "My husband did what your family did." "What part?" I asked her. She said he had left his hometown in the East, come to California, and passed. The only person in his West Coast life who knew he was black was his wife. I asked her if she had children, and did they know. "Yes, we have children, and no, they have no idea." She walked away easily with her signed book.

All of the people in my family who made the decision to pass are dead. I could not ask them about the issues they faced, the pain and anxiety they may have experienced, or their transition from marginality to centrality. My aunt would not talk about it. I suspect it was too emotionally freighted. After all, she lived all of her adult life as a white woman, married a white man, raised a white child, and became the grandmother of white grandchildren. To ask her to confront the enormity of that decision would have struck a blow at the very center of her self.

And so my aunt and I never discussed race, color, racism, discrimination, or prejudice. That is not to say that each time I was in her presence I did not have a secondary running dialogue just behind the real exchanges we were having. I wanted her to tell me what her life had been like keeping such an important—and to some, a dreadful—secret. But she was first and foremost my aunt, and I assumed a protective stance with her.

In the end, I did not bring up subjects that I knew would rip and tear at her core. I did not wish to do that. I wanted to find my mother's sister, and I did. I wanted to close the family circle, and I did. I wanted to lift my mother's burden, and I did. I wanted to graft the missing limbs back onto the family tree, and I did. I lifted my mother's burden. I wanted the grafts to "take," and they did.

Perhaps my age and experience have mellowed me. Had my recovery of my family happened when I was in my twenties or thirties, things might have turned out differently on all sides. Instead of reconciliation and joy, there might have been recrimination and anger. But I think I have learned well the lesson that venomous thoughts damage the thinker.

I look at my mother now, and I believe her *self* has changed. She has received a great deal of attention since her story was published. She has acquired many sympathetic fans and now acknowledges audiences with the practiced wave of royalty. She patiently signs autographs. For the first time in more than eighty years she receives communications from people who call her their aunt or, more important, their sister. She cannot let go her regrets about the missing years, but she views them with less bitterness, less anger, less sorrow. She has gained a new part of her self.

My sisters too have been changed by these events. They are pleased to see my mother happier. They are glad to have the information about their family, so that they can retain and pass on a more complete picture of where it is they came from. They too sorrow that they did not know their aunts and uncles, and that they missed some of the key years of their cousins. But they are determined to explore and enjoy this far-flung family well into the future. Make no mistake; this is just part of their lives. It is neither a major preoccupation nor a leitmotif. Finding Grace allowed us all to let go of the biggest issues, the longest shadows, and the deepest hurts.

We all say "if only," but then we move on because there are now more drawing rooms with variegated appointments in which to create our own newly expanded family drama. There is delight in discovering familial if not genetic similarities and strength in honoring the differences that our divergent histories have wrought.

Our children are more removed from the whole thing. It is they, perhaps, who can look at it most objectively. Among my siblings' children there has been a range of growing-up experiences. Some grew up in totally white towns, went to totally white schools, and in several cases married white spouses. Theirs is a more sanguine point of view. "What's the big deal?" they ask. For them, the racial line is no longer adamantine. It has been blurred and they do not work at re-creating it. They look back at the past with interest and curiosity, but, on the surface at least, they are free of the feelings that suffocated my mother's and my generation. Lucky for them.

The actions of my new relatives have been loving and positive. With more opportunities available to them than their forebears, those in the current generation include professionals, academics, and businesspeople. Some have lived as good, ordinary, struggling Americans. They have benefited from the built-in and often unconscious American privilege that goes along with skin that is thought to be white. Theirs is a complex and interesting story. Some of them will tell their story here.

As for me, I believe my *self* has expanded. The gift I presented my mother has been a gift to all of us. My soul is at peace. My black self has a new layer, but at this point, I am not sure what to call it.

All around us, perceptions of that thing we call race are sliding, shifting, tumbling. Thomas Jefferson had a black mistress and black children. Carol Channing, that flapper matchmaker and American blond icon, had a black father.

For most of his adult years, Anatole Broyard, the cultural critic of *The New York Times,* passed for white. His children would not know that he and they would have been considered black until he lay on his deathbed. His daughter, who grew up in the very white suburbs of Fairfield County, Connecticut, has been publicly exploring what it all means. She met many of her relatives on the "black" side of the family at a reunion in New Orleans, covered by Oprah Winfrey's *O* magazine.

We learned that the ultimate New York society maven of the '70s and '80s was passing. Add some high-profile types of mixed race: Mariah Carey, Vin Diesel, Tiger Woods, Halle Berry, Keanu Reeves, Norah Jones . . . the list grows every day. The dam has broken, and the stories of racial transformations pour forth.

In the meantime, efforts are being made to give a voice, a face, a context to that which has been among us since the Pilgrims arrived, if not the Spanish, the Italians, the Norse.

Trying to map out guidelines for people who prefer to follow the path of self-determination and self-identification, Maria Root, Ph.D., a scholar who writes about people of mixed race, presented a "Bill of Rights for Persons of Racially Mixed Ancestry" as part of a keynote address presented to a conference on multiraciality in 1993 at San Francisco State University. Her thirteen tenets were:

"WE HAVE THE RIGHT to change our identities from how our parents identify us.

"WE HAVE THE RIGHT to identify differently than our brothers and sisters.

"WE HAVE THE RIGHT to identify differently than other persons might identify us or expect us to identify.

"WE HAVE THE RIGHT to identify differently in different situations and know we are not mixed up, disloyal, or weak.

"WE HAVE THE RIGHT to change our identity over our lifetime—and more than once if need be.

"WE HAVE THE RIGHT to create a vocabulary to communicate about multiraciality because our language is not currently adequate.

"WE HAVE THE RIGHT to have loyalties and identification with more than one ethnic group.

"WE HAVE THE RIGHT not to fractionalize ourselves in order to conform to society's notion of race.

"WE HAVE THE RIGHT not to fit in exactly.

"WE HAVE THE RIGHT not to be responsible for people's discomfort with our presence and/or perceived ethnic ambiguity.

"WE HAVE THE RIGHT not to justify our existence or our identity choices.

"WE HAVE THE RIGHT not to justify our ethnic legitimacy.

"WE HAVE THE RIGHT not to engage in racially limited partnerships and friendships."

8

In the Best of Families

A PASSING STORY

"Long before Johnnie L. Cochran, Jr., and other black lawyers rose to prominence in California, there was Ernest J. Torregano," a prominent San Francisco lawyer who for years hid a secret from almost everyone who knew him. "Like Cochran, Torregano attained wealth and acclaim through the practice of law. Both were Louisiana natives who worked hard to build their careers and overcame racial barriers to achieve success." His death from a heart attack in 1954 was front-page news in the *San Francisco Chronicle.* This former president of the Lafayette Club, a social and charitable organization made up of Bay Area residents of French heritage (he had told people he was French) also became president of the San Francisco Planning Commission.

Before coming to San Francisco, Torregano married a woman of color from New Orleans, with whom he had one daughter. In New Orleans, the family was known as black, probably Creole. Torregano left his wife and family for work as a porter in San Francisco. He would return to New Orleans regularly to see his kin. In the meantime, in 1912 he enrolled in St. Ignatius College of Law. He established two mailing addresses, one in the black community and one in the white community. He sent home regular support checks to his wife and daughter. He told a friend at that time that he was "crossing over" to the white community.

Subsequently he finished and passed an examination, which admitted him to the bar. Believing that his wife and child had died in a fire, based on a story that his mother had told him, he married a white woman and severed all his remaining ties with his black origins in New Orleans. His brother Alfred had also come to San Francisco and was also passing while doing maintenance work. It was not until after Ernest died, some forty years later, that his true heritage came to light in a fierce probate fight. Ernest had willed his estate to his brother Alfred, but Ernest's long-lost daughter of color from New Orleans learned of his death and insisted on her rights as an heir to her father's estate. She won in court and received a third of the bulk of his estate.

(From "Before His Time," by Dick Goldberg,
Los Angeles Daily Journal)

Wellesley College in early June is a glorious, splendid place that hearkens back to 1870, when it was founded. The gentle green hills invite you to linger in their shadows and let the world beyond the campus slip away. Sometimes the sun blinds you as it bounces and dazzles off Lake Waban. Its ripples seemed unchanged since I first saw them in 1955, when I entered the college as a freshman. Gothic towers pierce the azure sky with elegant hauteur. In a low field across from the science complex, swaying flowering shrubs allow glimpses of feathery insects skimming the surface of Paramecium Pond, flying from water lily to water lily.

Everything seemed just as I remembered it—an idyllic place where idylls should be told. It was there I told mine.

I returned to Wellesley during a perfect spring weekend for my thirty-fifth reunion, as a keynote speaker for my class. Another keynoter that year was my classmate Madeleine Albright, then the United States ambassador to the United Nations. I had known Maddie well since our freshman year in college. She had lived next door to me in a small dormitory housing twenty-six women among whom I was the only black. We remained friends throughout our four years and kept in touch afterward.

Under a white tent on the great lawn bordering the stately quadrangle of dormitories known as Tower Court, after a New England dinner of lobster, steamed clams, and corn on the cob, I talked to my classmates and our spouses and friends about my family and its racial transformation. The all-white audience sat enthralled, almost in a state of wonder, at what they thought was a unique story. Many had never heard of the concept of "passing."

Ambassador Maddie held forth about the changes in the nation and the world. Once again, the listeners seemed rapt with admiration. Little did I know that four years later, Maddie, then secretary of state, might be able to address our class on the very same issue that I had covered, a family's passing. The shedding of one group identity for another. She had discovered hidden Jewish roots in her family tree.

During the Kosovo crisis, Maddie hosted me and some of our

other classmates and husbands at a fortieth reunion reception and dinner in Washington at the State Department and the Sulgrave Club, one of the city's preeminent clubs for women. When Maddie entered the Treaty Room, one of the State Department's elegant and formal reception areas, the freshmen within us escaped and exploded with the class cheer for 1959: "One-nine-five-nine, yellow shine fifty-nine, mighty fine, fifty-nine, one-nine-five-nine, Wellesley! Maddie, Maddie, Maddie!" Maddie giggled like the girl she had been. Radiantly happy, she was relaxed to be surrounded by those of us who had known her since she was eighteen years old. Neither the Balkan crisis nor her family's crossover saga intruded on our evening.

9

A Whiter Shade of White

A PASSING STORY

In the 1970s and '80s, Alice Mason's name was often in the
New York society pages. She traveled with the likes of all
those thin, rich society matrons who chair balls and lunch-
eons, and sit on boards and committees. According to
People magazine, Alice Mason, always described as a "New
York socialite" (few black ladies are ever described as
New York socialites), was confronted with the fact that
her father was a black dentist from Philadelphia. She also
had well-known and accomplished black relatives in New
York, including a niece who was highly placed in the
entertainment industry.

It is reported that Ms. Mason took the "outing" with
characteristic aplomb. She supposedly shrugged her ele-
gantly clad shoulders when she faced the truth of the mat-

ter with the statement that "many people had families who live on both sides of the color line." She went on to disclose that she "had lived this way for forty years" and that, for her, "race was a state of mind."

A state of mind, indeed. Good for you, Alice. I imagine that among those whites in her circle, always looking for the new, the exotic, the not-yet-experienced, the response was "How chic. How *je ne sais quoi.*"

Widely read newspaper columnist Bill Raspberry asked the question "Has America reached the point where most whites— where even a significant minority of whites—really don't care about race?" His answer: "Black Americans would respond with a resounding NO!"

Collaterally, a burgeoning interest in whiteness studies has developed. Some blacks are amused by the concept that people have just found out that they are white and are wondering what it *really* means. Some say they feel guilty about their whiteness and the privileges it has brought. Blacks, on the other hand, have been delving into what it means to be black or white ever since slavery days.

Recently, Maurice Berger, in his book *White Lies,* explored the subject of his own whiteness. It's as if whiteness were a newly sighted, accessible, but uncharted planet, steeped in exotically pale flora and fauna. Clearly, many believe that the unexplored subject of whiteness is rich and pregnant with possibilities, all sorts of permutations, combinations, and refutations. Some white people now affirm that they too are part of a defined group, they too can be seen as "the other." For some, that is a mind-bending revelation, an Einsteinian proposition. How they could have been moved from the center to the margin is a disturbing notion for many, and understandably so.

Margo Jefferson, Pulitzer Prize–winning columnist for *The New York Times*, keeps plumbing the depths of whiteness and near whiteness. The subject has her by the wrists and won't let go. She cannot finish with it. In columns about novelist Danzy Senza and actress Mary Pickford, Margo picks brilliantly at the deconstruction of whiteness. She examines every whiter shade of pale—or is it every paler shade of white? The issue of passing fascinates her, mesmerizes her, as revealed in a column about a Catholic woman who wrote a memoir about discovering her Jewish roots.

Margo Jefferson underlines and italicizes the fact that these racial and ethnic crossovers, while old stories, have new incarnations that involve hundreds of thousands of people.

In the waning months of 2002, much hoopla surrounded the removal of French/black novelist Alexandre Dumas's body from one grave to another, more-celebrated burial spot. The relocation was ordered by the French government in recognition of what Dumas, the son of a Haitian woman and a Frenchman, has meant to French literature and culture. To their credit, the French have taken his blackness for granted.

Just as the artist Edgar Degas had a black branch in his family, a branch that in itself had a rift between its light-skinned members and their browner brethren, so too are there many mixed living descendants of other famous and not-so-famous American and European folk. Rarely is it noted that John James Audubon, the painter whose exquisite renderings of birds are unrivaled, had a black Caribbean parent. What would that say about a partially black aesthetic—or would it be sensibility—that informed his artistic genius? No other artist has ever been able to match Audubon's verisimilitude of bird painting.

The year 2002 seemed to have been a watershed for these matters, as several British newspapers reported the old news that Queen Charlotte, the wife of King George III (who was on the throne at the time of the American Revolution), grandmother of Queen Victoria, and the direct ancestor of the current British monarch, Queen Elizabeth, had black heritage on her mother's side coming out of Portugal. Often called the "monkey-faced princess," Charlotte produced fifteen children with her husband. When the stories about Charlotte's heritage surfaced again, there was a flurry of interest for a few days, and then the media dropped the matter.

It seems that it was too much to bear to think that the British monarchy, the ultimate icon of whiteness, could possibly be black. Heaven forbid. What would everybody in the world *think*? They would have some context if they had read the story in a 1999 issue of London's *Sunday Telegraph* quoting a leading British geneticist as saying that at least one Briton in five has black genes, making some 11 million ostensibly white Britons the racial kin of Afro-Caribbeans. Would that mean, as columnist William Raspberry asked, "that these 11 million Britons are black? Does it mean they would be subject to 'outing' if their DNA became known? Or does it, as seems to be the reaction in Great Britain, mean nothing at all?" As Raspberry went on to say, "White racists created the absurd notion that blackness could not be diluted away by any amount of whiteness, while a single drop of black blood could render you and your descendants black forever."

10

The Indian Who Wasn't

A PASSING STORY

One of the most enduring and beloved images in America is the Indian head on the nickel coin. Another enduring Indian image is that of Espera DeCorti, born on the edge of a Louisiana swamp in 1904 to Italian immigrants Francesca Salpietra DeCorti, and Antonio DeCorti, who had come to New Orleans around the turn of the century. The dark-haired, dark-skinned Francesca was from a family of Sicilian wine growers. Espera, Francesca's son and the second of four children, went west. In Hollywood, without the benefit of a nose job or other plastic surgery, he became Iron Eyes Cody, America's favorite Indian icon, star of the movie *Sitting Bull.*

Iron Eyes Cody was best known nationally for his public service billboards as the chiseled, stoic Indian who, with a single large tear coursing down his leathery cheek, commented thunderously without words as he surveyed America's environmental transgressions. During his entire career, his family, his friends and acquaintances, some in the movie industry, and even some Indians knew and kept the secret of his Italian heritage. In fact, they were outdone when the newspapers outed Iron Eyes after his death in 1999. The supporters of Cody said he made a "perfectly good Indian" and represented the best qualities of Indian culture.

Race and its role in forming the American persona will not go away. Ralph Ellison nailed it. Richard Wright pierced it. Presciently, James Baldwin ground it up and spit it out, over and over. So have Studs Terkel, Cornell West, Tom Wolfe, Bill Bradley, Jamaica Kinkaid, Toni Morrison, "Skip" Gates, and numerous others. It is a story that will never go out of fashion. It will never be yesterday's news. Too many people are fascinated and frightened by it. Everyone wants to read about it, to know about it, to thrill and chill and titillate himself or herself by looking in the pier glass and wondering about it. To go to sleep dreaming about it, but nonetheless be relieved to wake up white.

For too many, being white will always be the American dream. For too many, waking up black will always be the American nightmare.

11

Tracking Will

It was a flawless spring day in 1995 on the island of St. John in the Virgin Islands. Dressed in colorful flowery prints, gauzy voiles, and wispy silks suitable for the tropics, my mother, my daughters, Melissa and Deirdre, my sister Pattee, and my husband, Harold, and I drove in an open lorry to Hawk's Nest Beach, a quiet inlet next to the larger, better-known Rockefeller Resort Beach, Caneel Bay. We laughed as my mother's fine hair blew over each side of her face like the ears of a springer spaniel. Initially, she was not thrilled with the prospects of the proceedings. She had never been to a wedding on a beach. Should she leave her shoes on? Was it okay to wear sunglasses? Where would the altar be? Where would she sit? Wouldn't sand get in the organ?

As it turned out, there was no altar, no organ, and we did not sit. We stood on crystalline sand. With the jewellike Caribbean as the backdrop, a local clergyman-turned-entrepreneur officiated at the marriage of Jeffrey Taylor, my brother's son, whose mother, Maureen, was an Irish woman from Malden, Massachusetts, to a white southern belle from Texas. Her mother, her mother's boyfriend, and her grandfather flew to the Islands for the nuptials.

Jeffrey, great-great-grandson of Edward Everett Morris, who had married the Irishwoman Margaret Maher, not only looked a great deal like his ancestor but was adding new yet similar genes to the family chromosomal complexity.

On this once slave-dominated island, a thousand miles away from the continental United States, my nephew was repeating the marriage pattern that had created one of America's new families more than a century before.

Jeffrey and his bride to be had fallen in love in modern-day Boston. He was marrying a woman whom he once legally could not have wed in America. She was marrying a man who came from a group that some of her Southern forebears probably routinely despised. But that day, none of the past mattered. The sky was blue, the ocean was turquoise, and the mountains were emerald. That day, only the sand was near white.

In a riotous potpourri of outfits and skin colors, we posed for wedding pictures against the brilliant sky. Brown and tan and cream and ivory, we joined hands. The warm wind blew our hair. The timid waves lapped our feet. The setting sun toasted our limbs.

In the end, Mother converted to modernism. She relaxed and opened herself up to the joy of the ceremony and the lively reception that followed in an open-air Caribbean courtyard. We all hoped that the spirits of Margaret Maher and Edward Everett Morris had crossed the ether to bear witness to their descendants' promise.

※

I was invited to speak at Salisbury University on the Eastern Shore of Maryland. Following the lecture, a dinner reception was planned. Mrs. Frank Perdue, the most famous and leading social denizen of the town, was the hostess. She had offered to host the party because she had learned that my grandfather, Will Morris, had worked for her husband's family's chicken business.

During his employment for the Perdue family business, Will had seen her husband grow from young boy to chief executive officer of a business that had begun as a local affair and become one of the nation's largest chicken-selling concerns. Frank Perdue achieved national celebrity as the country's chief chicken hawker on television. Some said that with his wiry frame and long neck, he looked like the product he sold.

The subtext for me was that my grandfather had been a low-status, low-paid hand on the chicken farm. Moreover, he had been passing for white. Now here I came, some sixty years later, to speak at the local university and be hosted by my grandfather's employer, who would have had no reason to have my grandfather in the social areas of his house. I understood that.

I had mixed feelings about going to Salisbury. My parents had impressed upon me that beyond the black beaches of Highland and Arundel, Maryland's Eastern Shore had long been an unwelcoming and dangerous place for black people. They never went into those hinterlands. Nor did they give me the particulars.

By 1931, the Eastern Shore had had thirty-one recorded lynchings since 1882. In 1931, the *Afro-American* newspaper had a year-long campaign against Salisbury, calling it "Maryland's Lynch Town" because of a particularly brutal lynching that had occurred there.

According to contemporaneous press reports, black Matthew Williams, described as a "quiet, industrious box and crate factory worker" and his white employer, D. J. Elliott, were in a room together and two shots were fired. No one else was in the room to witness the incident. Both men were wounded and taken to the local hospital. The white man died from his gunshot wound.

In an orgy that attracted two thousand people, a mob extracted Matthew from the hospital, hanged him from a tree in the front of the courthouse, burned him, cut him down, dragged his body behind a truck to the black part of town, and hanged him again—this time from a lamppost.

After about five hours, the Salisbury police retrieved the body and took it to some local woods, where they covered it with burlap and leaves. Within a few hours, the officials changed their minds, uncovered the body, and turned it over to a local black undertaker.

The story of the atrocity and the lawlessness was picked up by other newspapers and attracted considerable attention.

Two years later, in 1933, history would repeat itself in the town of Princess Anne, where twenty-two-year-old, learning-impaired George Armwood, accused of attacking a white woman, was retrieved from the jail and had his ear cut off by a teenager as he was pulled down the jailhouse steps. They tied him behind a car and dragged him down the street and across a field, where they found an appropriate tree to hang him using telegraph wire. While his body was twitching and swinging from the tree, men and women took turns beating him with various objects. They cut him down and brought his body back to the street, where they burned it, but not before retrieving a number of gold teeth from his mouth. This lynching too attracted a great deal of press attention.

These were the stories my parents lived with, the stories that kept them from the Eastern Shore, although my mother knew that her passing dad lived there. I did not know the details of such lynchings until I was old enough to read for myself the accounts in the black press. They left an indelible impression, one that made me wonder why my grandfather had chosen to live on the Eastern Shore in the first place.

For a majority of its residents, this rural area held only the promise of drudgery, mainly for unskilled labor. It is true that aside from his work as a liveryman, Will Morris had no other skills. And his alcoholism made him unreliable. He had to have known of the fear that area of the state engendered in black people. He had to have known of the lynchings and beatings of the colored citizens routinely unpunished and inaccurately reported in the small-town local papers of the area.

It might have been a cunning choice on his part, because he knew that few, if any, black outsiders, some of whom might have known him from Washington, would come his way. It was unlikely that they would show up in that unwelcoming place. As the *Baltimore News* said in a 1933 editorial against lynching, there was an "Eastern Shore horror. . . . and those guilty of the outrage against the peace and good name of the State of Maryland are left to their consciences and whatever steps will be taken by the legal authorities to punish them."

Other contemporaneous press headlines of the time exhorted, "Hang the Beast," "Make Them Answer," "Bestiality," "Eastern Shore — Jungle Spot," "Sheer Savagery," "Everything Except Eat Him," "A Mob Killed — The State Is an Accomplice," "Atrocities and Mob Law Too Prevalent."

The Eastern Shore grotesqueries resulted in the NAACP asking President Franklin Roosevelt to speak out against lynchings. The Washington, D.C., Women's International League requested that the president encourage antilynching legislation. The Communists joined the clamor, arranging protest meetings against the Eastern Shore lynchings. Yet this monstrous place was my grandfather's chosen sanctuary.

I developed a morbid fascination with the possibility that my grandfather, as a white man, might have witnessed a lynching on the Eastern Shore. It was quite possible. According to Leon Litwack's *Trouble in Mind* and contemporaneous press reports, often the whole town would be alerted that a lynching was going to occur and would turn out for the so-called barbecue parties. There have been stories of black men passing for white who witnessed such events and then reported them to the appropriate authorities. One such famous witness was Walter White, the NAACP leader.

As far as I know, Will Morris offered no such testimony. He continued to live on the Eastern Shore until he died.

One of the Salisbury College officials drove me around town and showed me the original chicken plant in which my grandfather had worked. It was a pitiful, rusty ruin. Thankfully, the stench of dead foul had long departed. I asked my aide to help me locate both Will Morris's death certificate, which I had never seen, and any obituary that might have been published.

While I was going about my academic foray, my new colleague did her research and came up with both the death certificate and the obituary. It was no surprise to me that the death certificate listed my grandfather as white and his birthplace as Virginia, neither of which was correct. His Irish mother's name, Margaret Maher, was correctly listed, but his mulatto father's name, Edward Everett Morris, was listed as Robert Morris.

In the obituary from the *Salisbury Times*, his survivors included his daughter, Grace Cramer of Cleveland, and his son, William Morris, Jr., also of Cleveland, three grandchildren, and three great-grandchildren. His daughter, my mother, Margaret Morris Taylor, her children, and his grandchildren were not listed or accounted for in the obituary. I did not share this document, which came into my life too late to be good news, with my mother. Why burden her with this absolute and crushing rejection of her existence in print?

Mrs. Perdue's party was a grand affair for a place like Salisbury. She and Frank lived in the manicured part of town, large homes with sweeping lawns. An artist whose specialty was decorating and sculpting goose eggs, she had read *The Sweeter the Juice* closely and had excerpted lines that she thought were special, enlarged them, and strung them around the rooms in which were also exhibited various examples of her goose egg art.

Mrs. Perdue had thoughtfully handpicked her crowd so that there would be an equal number of blacks and whites. Most of the folks knew only those whose skin was the color of their own. Several told me it was the first time a social party of that type had been held in Salisbury, and they hoped it wouldn't be the last. Frank, looking just like he did on television, sort of hung back.

In some ways, what an odd, almost zany happenstance it was. After all, here I was, the granddaughter of a black chicken laborer who had passed for white, returning to an area that was notorious for its venomous history with black people, to be entertained by the local queen of white society, the wife of the chicken entrepreneur who probably would not have let my grandfather in his front door, not because of his race but because of his class. The evening was pleasant enough, though, and I became a fan of the egg artistry.

The next day, I went to the local gift shop where the eggs were featured and acquired two for my collection. The previous evening I had told Mrs. Perdue that I wanted to commission her to create some "ancestor" eggs for me: miniature parlors with pictures of my restored family around the rooms.

As I was leaving the shop with two large, awkward, but lightweight boxes, several elderly white gentlemen sitting in the afternoon sun doffed their well-worn white straw hats and offered to help me carry my packages to the waiting car.

Instantly, something transported me back in time on that main street of Salisbury, and I envisioned the young black man swinging from the tree and then from the lamppost. I could not help but wonder if those elderly gentlemen had as young men been present at the lynching. Politely refusing their assistance, I struggled to the car with my packages. Then I felt guilty about my unkind and probably unjustified thoughts directed at those ostensibly courtly old men. Nonetheless, "the Eastern Shore" is a phrase that still creates dread in my heart.

It is difficult for me to make peace with the idea that my light-skinned grandfather, who had abandoned my mother, had chosen to live in a geographic environment that was not only hostile to but also deadly for black men. The idea was repulsive to me, especially since it was during a period when my dark-skinned father was making his way through the North and the South, fighting visibly for civil rights. After my father passed through New Jersey by car heading southward, he was always in a precarious position. He never knew when some good ole boy or vigilant Southern policeman might stop his car for no reason. And there was no guarantee as to what might happen next.

Grace Morris Cramer,
circa 1920.

My mother's elegant uncle
Edward Morris, who lived
in Buffalo.

Sumner Morris (second from left),
my mother's brother, who survived World
War I but who never saw my mother again.

Edward Morris, my
mother's brother, who died
of influenza in World War I.

Edward Everett Morris, son of a judge and a house slave; Margaret and Grace's grandfather, my great-grandfather; circa 1867.

Will Morris as a boy; son of Edward Everett Morris, father of Margaret and Grace.

Will Morris as a liveryman, in his prime.

Will Morris, the grandfather I never knew, at eighty.

✳ Mother (front row, left) in her New Haven Links club.

Mother ✳ (third from left) in her Ansonia, Connecticut, College Club.

✳ My Taylor siblings and me with our spouses, celebrating our parents' thirty-fifth anniversary.

✳ Patricia Cramer Scott, the
cousin I never knew. Grace's
only daughter and the mother
of Jeff, Laura, and Lisa Scott,
she died prematurely.

✳
Jewelle (right) and
me (middle) with
Carol Morris Battles, the
cousin I found and cherish.

✳
Mother surrounded by her
sister's grandchildren (left to
right): Laura Scott Hoover,
Jeff Scott, and Lisa Scott.

Jeff Scott, Margaret's great- ✳
nephew, embracing his aunt
and his grandmother.

Sisters together again. Margaret
(standing) and Grace, who both
love cats.

Two sisters walking from the
past into the present on the
day they met after a seventy-
six-year separation.

Making friends of relatives. Melissa
and Grace, niece and great-aunt.

My cousin Dorothy Morris
Dunker and me, meeting for the
first time in Minneapolis.

The Minnesota cousins: (front) Anthony Miccio; (second row, from left) Glen Dummer, Donna Dunker Dummer, Dorothy Morris Dunker; (third row, from left) Amelia Wherland, Delana Dummer, Kirsten Bourke, Darcy Dummer Miccio; (back row, from left) Chris Dummer, Greg Dummer, Brad Pace.

The Hoffman cousins (left to right): Jeff, Trisha, Les, Barbara, Kevin.

Mother meeting her great-niece Darcy Miccio Pace for the first time.

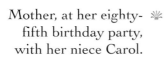

Mother, at her eighty-fifth birthday party, with her niece Carol.

✻ Dustin and Linda Suits, cousins from Illinois who, like us, are descended from Judge Halyburton's family.

✻

Mother with her granddaughter Julie, and Julie's groom, Drew Massey.

My husband, ✻ Harold, with my cousins Carol and Glen Battles, in North Haven, Connecticut.

✻

Mother on the beach with her children and grandchildren at her grandson Jeffrey's wedding in St. John, U.S. Virgin Islands.

❋ My sister Jewelle and her husband, Jim, with Jeff Scott and Peggy and Jan Santos, San Francisco cousins.

❋

My sister Pattee and my mother riding to the *Oprah* show in one of Oprah's limos.

❋

An Oprah moment—after the show, cousins socializing for the first time (from left to right): Carol; her daughter Peggy; Jewelle; and Donna Dummer, Dottie's daughter.

❋

My mother with most of her grandchildren at her eighty-fifth birthday party.

12

Life Review

A PASSING STORY

Adrian Piper, an artist and philosophy professor at Wellesley College, wrote about part of her family that had passed.
The story began, "Once, long ago, there was a woman who
was very beautiful, intelligent and strong-willed. She was
one of five sisters, all beautiful, intelligent and strong-willed,
all competing with one another, all school teachers before
they married.

"Her father was a minister, a tall, handsome, charis-
matic man who later lost his faith and became a lawyer.
Her mother was a local beauty, temperamental and impe-
rious. The woman's family was a very important one
where they lived, and very proud and well to do. They
were not quite white. But they were all very fair-skinned,
pale and pink, with visible blue veins in their hands and
wrists, amber eyes and wavy auburn hair. . . ."

Piper went on to say that the woman had one daughter who went away to Ivy League undergraduate and graduate schools, became a professional, married a successful white professional, and apparently passed for white. Piper confided that she has never gotten over the hurt caused by the fact that those who were passing would not get in touch with her or the rest of the family. Piper wrote, "She tried to imagine what it must be like to hate that coldly, to want to disown one's family, entirely, absolutely and forever." Piper recalls the funeral of her father: "At the funeral mass, many were wondering whether the dead man's sister would appear. His wife and daughter, grief stricken and stung by her hardness, doubted it. But midway through the service, a small, pale young woman tiptoed into the church. She had a profile her relatives recognized from the newspaper photographs of her father. Her gaze swept the faces—tan, brown, black, white—of the congregation, before she sat down, blushing, in an isolated corner pew. The object of intense scrutiny from the dead man's family and friends, she kept her face averted, and tiptoed out before the service came to an end. Afterward, the dead man's daughter wrote to thank her cousin for coming, and mentioned that they had attended the same university at the same time, but received no reply."

> *(From "A Tale of Avarice and Poverty" by Adrian Piper,*
> Whitewalls, *winter 1987)*

For a few weeks after Grace's death, my mother stayed with me in California. There was time for us to reflect on the past and the present. In a series of chats in the garden, I asked my mother how she now looked at everything that had happened. How did she feel about it? Had her ideas about the shape of her past changed? Was she happy that she had found her family and that they had claimed her? What difference did her "new family" make to her, a woman in her mideighties, who for more than seventy-five years had lived with the ghosts of her kin?

"I still have feelings about it. I will always be a little sad, I guess," she said. "I still get angry with my father, but I understand better now what happened. He couldn't take care of me and the rest of the family." She was especially forgiving of Grace. "She was just a girl who faced a more difficult life than I did. She knew she could not rely on her father, who she followed around. Her life did not settle down until she lived near our grandmother and our brother Bill in Buffalo and Cleveland. And my brother Bill, he did the best he could taking care of Grace and my other brothers. I just feel so bad we missed all those years."

I thought I perceived a type of calmness, an air of quiet liberation about my mother in the years after we found her family. It was if she had become a whole, centered person who could locate herself in an extended family album. And she finally *knew* what had happened. Hearing the story directly from Grace linked her to the voices of her brothers, the voice of her father, the voice of her grandmother, the voices of her aunts and uncles. Seeing her father's handwriting and reading the letters he had written to Grace over the years animated the cardboard figure that had been her father. In her mind's eye she could contextualize the lives of Grace, her brother Bill, and her father, Will.

When Bill's great-granddaughter Darcy had an engagement party in Orange County, California, she invited us to come. My mother was the family matriarch of the event. Darcy was marrying into an Italian family, some of whose skin color reflected the range of hues found in Mother's darker world.

Delighted that my mother was present, Darcy took her by the hand. They wandered throughout the house and out onto a candlelit terrace hugging a dramatically lit swimming pool as Darcy introduced Mother to all the guests as her great-great-aunt. What a lovely moment it was for my mother to be the center of this, her family.

Wherever I took my mother as I spoke about her story, she was shyly delighted and flattered that people would approach her with a mixture of curiosity, interest, and sympathy. Those who turned out for lectures or book signings could not resist hugging her, patting her arm, stroking her back, and asking her all sorts of personal questions about her family. And they told her their stories and their troubles. Ever smiling, she listened patiently with kindness and compassion. They sensed that, and it endeared her even more to them.

During that period, Grace was still guarded. With my mother and me, at least, she did not go into the circuitous subtleties of race as it had affected her. Like my mother, Grace was a forgiving soul. She still spoke with great affection about her Irish grandmother, Margaret Maher, and her father, Will, and her brother Bill, with whom she had lived when she first moved to Cleveland from the East Coast. They remained patron saints of her heaven, with her father always being the tipsy angel. She told us that she had often visited her father when he lived on the Eastern Shore. She said what she liked most and remembered best about the visits was the seafood.

It was clear that discussion of the racial androgyny of her family was in a realm that Grace did not wish to visit. She welcomed all of my mother's family whom she met, but her natural reserve limited her curiosity about their lives. In her mind it seemed as if they simply were who they were. In the broader sense, that was quite lovely. Grace looked over the wall of skin color and saw in the garden only character and personality. Unwittingly, she practiced what America preaches.

Because of her age and general reclusiveness, Grace had few friends at the point in her life when she met her sister, me, and the other members of our family. There were a nearby neighbor, and a former coworker, and Christmas card friends in Cleveland, where she had lived before moving to Anaheim.

This tiny circle of friends precluded a tsunami of curiosity from overwhelming her. And unless they watched *Oprah*, I doubt they even knew that Grace's life had taken on a new dimension. She did not tell them. As had been her practice for so many years, she kept her counsel. I believe the only one Grace may have had conversations with about the dramatic changes in her life was herself. After I returned from the book tour of *The Sweeter the Juice*, I found a letter waiting for me from Aunt Grace. Expecting to be upbraided, I was relieved and surprised at its contents.

Dear Shirlee,
I haven't heard from you in weeks. When are you coming down to visit again? I miss seeing you. Please call and come visit soon.

Love, Aunt Grace

13

Eyes Other than Our Own

A PASSING STORY

In 1796, Michael Morris Healy was born in County Roscommon, Ireland. After deserting from the British Army in Canada during the War of 1812, he immigrated to Georgia, in the country near Macon. With the luck or skill of the Irish, he came into possession of a plantation said to have had more than a thousand acres with many, many slaves. Sometime during the latter part of the 1820s, he had a sexual relationship with a mulatto girl, a teenager at the time, named Mary Eliza Smith. They had ten children, all publicly claimed and recognized by Healy. Because of Georgia law, Healy could not marry or free the mother of his children, nor could he free his children. Instead, he sent them north for freedom and education. The children lived up to their father's hopes, all passing as white, most achieving great accomplishments.

The oldest son, James Augustine Healy (1830–1900)

enrolled at Holy Cross in Worcester, Massachusetts, along with his brothers. He became the first black Roman Catholic priest and the first black bishop of Portland, Maine, although it was assumed he was white. (The bishop who had facilitated Healy's career, John Fitzpatrick of Boston, knew of Healy's black heritage but did not reveal it.)

Patrick Francis Healy (1834–1910) a Jesuit, became the president of Georgetown College in Washington, D.C., in 1874, the first black president of a white college in the United States. At the college, he had previously served as a philosophy professor and vice president. Few if any people knew at the time that Patrick was black.

Michael Healy (1839–1904) became a high-ranking officer in the United States Revenue Cutter Service, a forerunner of the Coast Guard. He led a colorful life, and some believe he was the model for the hero in Jack London's *The Sea-Wolf*, as well as a character in James Michener's *Alaska*.

Four of the Healy sisters became ostensibly white nuns.

Before Oprah Winfrey initiated her television book club, she invited me and ten members of my Taylor and Morris families to discuss our story on her hourlong television show. We appeared for most of the scheduled hour, and some of us met each other for the first time. Oprah had also invited an expert, Professor F. James Davis, who had written a well-known book on race called *Who Is Black?*, to offer information about an area he had studied extensively.

The show was neither sensational nor exploitative and was laid out as an academic exercise—a look into one family's history across color lines and down through the generations.

That day I met my cousins Carol Battles from Ohio and Donna Dummer from Minnesota, and Carol's daughter, Peggy, from San Francisco. Grace's grandson, Jeffrey Scott, was present and was an eloquent, compelling spokesman for the West Coast contingent. Attentive, perky, and curious in their posture under the television lights, the Morris family members exhibited only positive responses to the news that their genealogy included black heritage. To a person, no one suggested or even hinted that being part black was a negative or a bad thing.

The consensus on the show was that the two sides of the family seemed delighted with each other and exhilarated to explore familial similarities and differences. I think this shook America up. Traditionally, black people had always been told that if their white relatives learned of their black heritage, they would become depressed to the point of being suicidal. This was always an effective deterrent to keep the curious from reaching out and crossing over the racial border. No one wanted to be guilty of prompting someone to jump out of a window or swallow a bottle of aspirin.

On the day the show aired, there was a major snowstorm in the Midwest and the East, causing many people to stay home from school and work. Oprah's audience on that snowy afternoon swelled beyond its usual numbers. Her production aides subsequently informed us that our show had been one of the most popular of her series and one that generated a flood of letters. Now in syndication, it is often selected for replays around the world.

The power of television is unsettling. Wherever we went after *Oprah*, whether in malls, movie houses, or colleges or on the street, people not only recognized us from the program but also had a lot to say about its contents. We became a mobile oral history facility, listening to other people's stories about passing, family secrets, and family separations.

In a supermarket line, an old gentleman turned around and said to my husband, Harold, "Weren't you on the *Oprah* show, talking about some of your white relatives you met on an airplane?" And in a mall outside Los Angeles, two black sisters walked by the table where my mother and I were signing autographs. They giggled and backed up. One looked at my mother and said, "You're the black sistah from the *Oprah* show, aren't you?" My mother smiled and affirmed the question, "Yes, I'm the black sistah."

14

Unexpected Encounters
of Kith and Kin

My family's story serves as a fulcrum for dialogues and meditations about race, identity, and family. It is a set of scales that measure not justice but humanity; not skin tone but timbre of character; not the social construct of race but the blood and bone of family.

From blacks, Jews, uncategorized whites, whites who think they may be mixed, and whites who wished they were, the letters about my mother's story came in droves. Each letter is a jewel of a story unto itself, some bitter, some sweet, all pieces of that heap of mountains, fields, valleys, cities, and towns we call America. All reflecting the larger story of America's obsession with and repression of race. All seen through one family's lens, up close and personal.

And the stories from tearful, profoundly moved, earnest people all along the racial front came verbally, in person, or over the phone. In airports, on airplanes, in bookstores, university classrooms, coffeehouses, malls, churches, synagogues, women's meetings, and professional conventions, my mother's story touched a large, communal nerve in America causing wildly ranging emotions and revelations.

In Seattle I encountered a man who called himself "the dean of Seattle's broadcasters." Years ago he had obviously fallen in love with the sound of his admittedly silken, deep voice. Ostensibly white and in his sixties, he told me on the air that except for the color of his grandfather's skin, he had always thought his grandfather had what he described as "Negroid features." When he added that his grandfather's first name was Washington, I opined, "I hate to tell you this, but I never knew any white family that named its children Washington. Where I come from, that was always a popular name with black people." I did not mean to say that everyone with the name Washington was black, just those in my part of the country. Without success he tried to hide his confusion. He said he was going to check the census information on his grandfather in the next few weeks.

At a book signing in a Southern California shopping mall, a stylish forty-something woman with natural dark red hair and amber eyes shared her confidence. "I understand this story, because it happened in my family. But it stopped with my father." I was curious about this gene stoppage and intrigued by this woman's unconscious denial of part of her heritage. "You see," she continued, "I was raised white here in California, but when I went to Texas for Founders' Day in my hometown, I saw a picture of my great-grandmother for the first time. There was no doubt about it, she was colored. There was no way she could even pass for Indian. I was told she died after giving birth to my grandfather. When my father was born, nothing was ever said about his heritage. So everything stopped with him." I did not feel it was incumbent on me at that time and at that place to review the matter of how chromosomes and genes pass along from one generation to the next.

Denial comes in infinite versions. Some are not subtle. In Boston, I knew there was no balm I could offer the black man with freckles, green eyes, and blondish-brown hair — the tightly coiled hair some call "rhiney and kinky" — clutching my book to the middle of his chest as if protecting an ancient wound that would not heal. He told me that as an eight-year-old holding his mother's hand walking in the streets of St. Louis on a summer afternoon, he would never forget an aborted encounter. An apparently white man came strolling toward the boy and his mother. As the three drew close enough to see one another's faces, the boy's mother began to tremble violently. That same moment, the man bolted and ran across the street, sprinting around the corner and out of sight.

At that point in his story, the book holder took a deep breath, clearly close to tears. "My mother, who was also light skinned, had turned red and was crying silently as she looked at the corner where the man had just vanished. 'That was my brother,' she said. 'He's passing and I haven't seen him in twenty-two years.' That was their last encounter. I never saw him again. But I will never, ever forget the deep pain and the tears on my mother's face."

Chicago welcomed me during one of its coldest winters. Only a little less frigid was the greeting from the media aide assigned to me during my visit, who met me at the airport. The young woman, a debutante type usually called Muffie or Buffie, quickly and with some reserve and in the Chicago version of Locust Valley lockjaw, informed me that she had graduated from Princeton and that her brothers, father, and grandfather also had graduated from Princeton. I thought surely that she would add that her great-grandfather had founded Princeton, but she didn't.

On our second day together, her personal freeze began to thaw. Now animated, she said that in reading my book while waiting for me, she had just discovered that she was probably related to me.

How's that?" I asked. "Well, I see that you are related to Martha Washington and so am I, so I guess that makes us distant cousins." She continued, "When I told my father about it last night, he was excited until I got to the part about your being black." Then he said, 'Maybe this explains that lost branch Aunt Suzie hasn't been able to find.'"

Sitting cross-legged on the floor in front of a signing table at the end of a passageway that led to a bookstore in a mall in Orange County, a cherubic curly-haired young woman brought to mind images of a beautiful Romanian Gypsy. When she spied my mother approaching in my wake, the dark-haired girl sprang to her feet, grabbed my mother's hand, and began sobbing, deep, woeful, stomach-twisting sobs. My mother, who wears her emotions just under her skin, also began to cry. Seeing this stranger and my empathetic mother holding hands and weeping, I too began to cry. There we were, a mother, a daughter, and a woman unknown to either of us, wailing as if we were professional mourners at an Irish funeral. After parking the car, Harold walked up and thought we had been mugged. Finally, the young woman cleared her last sob and poured out her story.

She had grown up a member of the only Jewish family in her small town in Orange County. Scarred by the prejudice she experienced as a child because she did not have the iconic California straight blond hair and blue eyes, she decided to hide her Jewish heritage. She would become a Gentile. She straightened and dyed her hair, bobbed her nose, changed her name, and left both Orange County and her Jewishness behind.

But, she told my mother, the break with her family had done her more harm than good. She recanted her choice and returned to the bosom of her family and her religion. She could not "pass" any longer. Touched by the sorrow that passing had brought to my mother's life and to her own, she had come to the mall to empty her heart to my mother, face-to-face. She cried, she said, for the unrelenting pain they both knew.

That very same day in the same location, a light-skinned thirty-something black couple stopped to talk. Green eyes peered at my mother from under a neat, bobbed sandy brown hairdo. Touching my mother, the young woman cried quietly. What had happened to my mother had also happened to her mother, she said. Her mother had died sorrowfully, without ever reuniting with her family. The young woman wanted to "see" another woman who had lived through and triumphed over an experience that her own mother had left unresolved. The daughter wanted to experience vicariously my mother's gift.

It was clear to me now that my mother, who had once been the psychological repository of blackness for her white family, had become a beacon of light for those who wanted to reconnect with their families. She had become a touchstone of truth.

In the Point Loma section of San Diego, there is a vast bookstore that has been converted from one of the city's vintage theaters. Bordered in triple rows of Caribbean-colored neon light bars, the curving art deco outdoor marquee bore my name. In this arresting setting, an equally arresting, elegant, pale woman with large gray eyes and a croquignole wave pressed her business card into my hand. On one side was printed "ethnic hair specialist." On the other was a quickly scribbled note, "I will call you to tell you my story."

The next day, I heard her voice at the other end of the wire. As an adopted child, she had always wondered about her ethnicity because she did not feel she was either black or white. She had just managed to have her adoption records unsealed and had seen for the first time a picture of her long-dead mother: a teenage Jewish girl who had conceived an out-of-wedlock child by a young black man. The girl's family had prevailed on her to give the child up for adoption.

In the file was a letter from the mother saying that she wanted to reclaim her baby. She never did, seemingly because of the daunting process at that time. She later died in a mental institution. "You don't know what it meant to me as a grown woman to see my mother's face, to touch her handwriting, to learn that she really did want me, and to know about my mother." I knew.

Back in Los Angeles, I had an urgent telephone message that a young woman had to speak with me immediately. When I returned the call, the woman told me that she had not known she was black until she was twelve years old. Her hair was blond, her eyes green, and her skin fair. All her family had passed for white in San Diego.

And that's what she had assumed she was until the day she found an old family scrapbook with some yellowed photographs of people who were clearly brown. She asked her parents about them. Her mother refused to discuss the photographs or anything related to them; her father admitted they were relatives but said he had left "that life" behind on the East Coast.

At seventeen, the girl went east to meet some of her dark relatives, and upon returning to the West Coast she decided, she said, to "embrace her blackness." She was the only member of her family to do so, although the rest of her siblings had been informed of their heritage. Now the director of a large and flourishing human service facility in Watts, a once historic but rapidly changing African-American and Latino neighborhood in Los Angeles, she stays in touch with all of her family but lives on the darker side of the color line. Her mother refuses to join her there.

How would my story play out in the heart of Dixie? I wondered a little nervously while being driven to a radio interview on the far outskirts of Atlanta. The small-scale station occupied the second floor of a nondescript two-story, boxlike building. My interviewer, a heavyset, jovial, middle-aged man in a short-sleeved shirt, eyed me with a curiosity that matched my own. Yes, I thought, he does fit my image of a "good ole boy." Now what?

I sensed it was important to quickly establish common ground. I told my radio host that I had just visited another beautiful Southern area, Hertford, North Carolina, on the eastern end of the state where my father was born. "By Jiminy," he drawled, "I don't believe it. That's where I'm from. Isn't it truly God's country? Now, don't tell too many people about it, because we want to keep it small and secret. By Jiminy, I knew I was going to like you."

His interview was straightforward, with no blind curves or culs-de-sac. When it was over, I asked him how he thought white Southerners would respond. "Well, Shirlee," he said, "we've all known this for years. Some of the ole-timers may not like to see it in print, but what the heck, it's all part of that devilish thing we call history."

Early one Saturday morning, the graceful Southern voice of an elderly man told me on the telephone he was sorry to interrupt my weekend privacy, but he had just finished my book and could not wait until Monday to talk with me. He had called directory assistance for my telephone number.

Since regional accents often meld race, I couldn't tell whether he was black or white. He wanted to know more about my mother's Halyburton side of the family, which he had researched and said he was related to, thus making him distantly related to me. I was pleased to be able to supply him with facts about two Halyburton generations of which he had no knowledge, dating back to the late 1600s in Scotland. After we had talked a bit, he told me how close he felt to various aspects of my story, because like my father, he too was a Baptist preacher.

Always concerned about tact and diplomacy, I asked him what he called himself.

"My family is mixed, like yours, and I think of myself as a mulatto. I know I had two black aunts, but somehow we got whitah."

"What does your community call you?" I queried.

"Oh, white, of course."

"And your congregation?"

"They're white too."

The minister told me he lived in a small town in the Blue Ridge Mountain area of North Carolina and that he was going to preach about my story on Sunday.

The most intriguing revelation was from a woman who had discovered that not only did she have a parent and grandparents whom society would have considered black, but that her forebears had lived in an area encompassing corners of Virginia, West Virginia, and North Carolina famous for its mixture of black, white, and Indian.

The women's ancestors had lived in a town near the Underground Railroad that had been called New Africa until shortly after the Civil War, when the name and perhaps the race of the entire town had been changed. Most of the people in the town had light skin.

(I remembered reading something about a small group of all-black towns that had sprung up in the late nineteenth and early twentieth centuries as havens for black citizens. One such was Eighty Acres, New Jersey, now known as Elsmere, which has a very Southern feeling. Rosewood, Florida, a black town destroyed by white rage, was also one of those communities. Few of these towns retain their original ethnic homogeneity.)

For six years she pursued documentation of this town and finally found it among lists of Civil War–era school districts. She talked with newly discovered elderly relatives who never admitted to being "colored" but were clearly from the darker side of the equation, she thought. She has written an as-yet-unpublished book about the experience, titling it *The Last to Know*.

There is a bookstore in Washington—Vertigo; it's called—that specializes in books about people of color. At a crowded book signing there, attended mostly by black people, including many of my Washington relatives on my father's side and my husband's relatives as well, a young white woman who had been standing in the back of the store unobtrusively made her way to the signing desk. She looked at Harold and blurted out that she was sure she was related to him. Then she began to cry, as Harold's relatives surrounded her.

She told the story of reading *The Sweeter the Juice* in Hawaii, where her husband had been stationed in the military, and being piqued by the Haizlip connection. When they came back to the States, she asked her father about the family history in North Carolina. He told her that the papers were out in the garage. She found some old family genealogy charts and thought she saw the intersection where the two families had been one. Her father, she said, wanted nothing to do with the idea. She was thrilled with the prospects and wanted to know us. It was a deeply emotional moment reflecting what some might call a sea change.

The Haizlips had come from a hardscrabble part of the country where racial enmity was deep and bitter. Harold had grown up in a totally segregated environment in Washington, D.C. He recalled North Carolina summers where his entire demeanor and behavior had to change radically so that he could survive to return home to school in the fall. And now this white North Carolinian was claiming him.

Just before I began my presentation at a bookstore in Denver, the owner said she had had a telephone call from a man who was on his way, driving 150 miles to meet me, carrying papers that would "prove" that he was related to me but, more precisely, to the Haizlips. And he wanted me to know before he got there that he was "white."

As I finished my talk, a jolly-looking, rotund fellow who could have passed for Santa Claus's brother rushed in the door, beamed, and waved a large old book at me. He could not wait for me to see the Haizlip family ledger of names, dates, births, occupations, geographical locations, and other highlights, which he believed revealed our family connections. I embraced him and his book. What a lovely idea, I realized, to be related to people everywhere. It's just a down-to-earth reaffirmation of current scientific thought.

PART II

Relativity

15

In Their Own Voices

In October 2002, I wrote a letter to all of my immediate family and my "new family," asking them to share what was most significant to them about our reconnecting as family. Not everyone felt the need to reply. Of those who did, here are their replies, just as they were written.

DOROTHY MORRIS DUNKER

Dorothy Morris Dunker was born in the 1920s, the older of two daughters of my mother's brother Bill. She had no knowledge of his black heritage. She is my mother's niece and one of those first cousins I used to fantasize about when I was a child. I would not meet her until 1994. Dottie, as she is known, is a sweet, attractive woman who dotes on her children and grandchildren. She is a housewife who has lived in Minnesota for many years.

Dear Shirlee

How exciting, another book, and I love the title. Aunt Grace meant a lot to me in my younger years. So it will be a treat to read your *Finding Grace.* As to the impact on my life since *The Sweeter the Juice,* it has been to be in contact with stepsister, Carol. We have enjoyed visiting and corresponding throughout these years, including meeting each other's families. Meeting you and Harold and also Jewelle and Jim has been enlightening. I do look forward to seeing you again and to reading the new book.

Sincerely,
Dottie

JEWELLE TAYLOR GIBBS

Jewelle is my "big sister" and the oldest of my mother's children. She was born in the 1930s. Jewelle holds a Ph.D. and is a clinical consulting psychologist who recently retired from Berkeley as a professor holding an endowed chair. She is the author of four books, including Preserving Privilege: California Politics, Propositions, and People of Color *(2001) and* Race and Justice: Rodney King and O. J. Simpson in a House Divided *(1996).*

The call came on a sunny May morning in 1992 when I was finishing breakfast, rushing to visit my husband in the hospital. Jim was slowly recovering from surgery for prostate cancer, discovered while we were on sabbatical leave in Washington, D.C., ensconced in a comfortable town house on Capitol Hill. His surgery had been the only sour note in an otherwise stimulating and productive year that we had shared as Visiting Scholars, Jim at the Smithsonian Institution Human Studies Film Archives, and I at the Joint Center for Political and Economic Studies, also reconnecting with family and friends in the Washington area.

My sister Shirlee had come to stay with us for a week while she was conducting research at the National Archives and interviewing older relatives for her family memoir. On that particular morning, she was upstairs and answered the phone when it rang. Almost immediately I heard a loud shriek, followed by several muted exclamations of surprise, so I ran upstairs to see what had happened, fearing the worst news about my husband or someone else in the family. She had a stunned but happy look on her face and announced to me: "They've found Grace and she's alive and well." After a lifetime of fantasizing about my mother's older sister, Grace Morris Cramer, I was amazed that the private detective Shirlee had hired had actually located her. After hanging up the phone, Shirlee asked: "Can you guess where Grace is living—in Anaheim, the home of Disneyland and make-believe. Isn't that ironic?" That was one of many ironies we were to discover about our newly found "white" relatives over the next few months.

After we hugged each other and danced around the airy bedroom, I had two almost simultaneous thoughts: how will my mother react to this incredible news? And how will Grace respond to us? They had not seen each other since my mother was four and Grace was nearly 12, 76 years and a whole lifetime ago. Two sisters, separated by a continent between them, had lived their lives in black and white worlds, with no contact and no knowledge of the other's hopes and dreams, or trials and tribulations.

For the rest of that week our feelings alternated between euphoria and sober reality about the implications of finding

Grace. We were euphoric because we knew it would be the greatest gift we could give our mother for her upcoming 80th birthday, but we were also realistic that Grace wouldn't be overjoyed to be found and "outed" as a black person after living most of her life as white. Shirlee and I had different opinions about even contacting Grace, who was then in her late eighties. I was concerned that the shock might kill her, but Shirlee was determined to contact Grace and try to arrange a belated reunion between the two sisters, recalling how sad my mother always seemed at holiday time without any sibling, she would frequently say, "I wish I could see my sister Grace one more time before I die." I countered with the fear that we might be exposing our mother to the pain of further rejection, forcing her to relive the trauma of abandonment that she had experienced as a child when her father and Irish grandmother had conspired to separate her from her older siblings, who all were dispersed to live in the white world.

Earlier that spring, before the phone call that changed our lives, I had spent some time at the National Archives trying to fill in the gaps of my mother's murky heritage. My mother's paternal side of the family claimed that they were descended from the "First Families of Virginia," although as teenagers we had turned it into a joke about being descendants of the slaves of the first families of Virginia. It was only after I graduated from college and took my first job with the Labor Department in Washington that I learned from an older cousin that one of our white ancestors had been a well-known judge in Richmond, Virginia.

Many years later when we were living on the Stanford campus, I decided on a whim to check out the judge's name at the Law School Library and found that he was, indeed, a prominent U.S. District Court Judge. Shirlee's research would confirm this and further reveal that he had sworn in Jefferson Davis as the President of the Confederate States in February, 1861, shortly before the beginning of the Civil War. This legacy, however unpalatable to me, provided the impetus for years of archival research on our family history.

Later that spring, on a parallel track with Shirlee's pursuit, I picked up the search again at the National Archives, which was within walking distance of our townhouse. I was directed to the pre–Civil War Slave Records, which listed all the slaves by their owners' names and locations throughout the slave-holding states. After weeks of poring over the microfiche records for Henrico County, Virginia, I finally found the name of James D. Halyburton, with the list of slaves that he owned at his residence in Richmond. Quickly scanning the list, my heart nearly burst when I saw the entry for a "mulatto female slave, age 45." I knew instinctively that, though she was name-less, here was the documentary evidence of my great-great grandmother, the mother of Edward Everett Morris. Living in the Halyburton household, he had been named after one of the Judge's Harvard classmates, presumably with certain privi-leges accorded to him because of their special relationship. Shirlee's independent research confirmed my own.

On a hunch, I checked the names of the property owners who lived near the Halyburton residence and discovered that the Adolphus Morris family owned the adjacent prop-erty. Recalling that slaves usually took the name of their owners, I concluded that my great-great grandmother had come from the Morris estate, perhaps sold away because she was the owner's mulatto child, only to repeat the cycle all over again when she joined the Judge's household.

There was still more research to do in the spring of 1992 while I was on the East Coast. During a break from a meet-

ing of the Radcliffe Board of Trustees in Cambridge, I paid
a visit to the Widener Library Archives at Harvard University to seek more information about the Judge. Shirlee had
shared his prominently placed obituary from the Richmond
papers which chronicled his educational background and
career highlights. He had graduated from Harvard in 1823,
nearly 130 years before I took classes in the Harvard Yard
as a Radcliffe student in the early 1950's. Again, I was
incredibly lucky. I found an entry in his class yearbook and
a photograph of him at his 50th class reunion in 1873, just
six years before his death in 1879.

The final piece of the puzzle fell into place when one of
my Washington cousins, the daughter of the family historian, finally gave me formal photographs of my Mother's
paternal grandparents, Edward Everett Morris and his
Irish-born wife, Margaret Maher. In partial profile, the
photographs of Edward and Judge Halyburton bore a
striking resemblance to each other with their high fore-
heads and prominent long noses. Nearly a year later their
relationship would be essentially confirmed by a legitimate
heir of the Judge who contacted Shirlee to share photographs of his great-grandfather Peyton Halyburton. His
remarkable resemblance to our own great-grandfather supported our family's oral history that they were half-brothers
who had played together as children in the Judge's home,
only to be separated later by virtue of race and legitimacy.

Finding Aunt Grace launched me on a journey to help
find my mother's lost relatives and took me to three continents in search of our family roots. It began on the *Oprah*
show in February, 1993. Her staff orchestrated the reunion
of my mother with one of her nieces, two great-nieces and
one great-nephew, in front of a worldwide viewing audi-

ence. My two sisters and I flew to Chicago and, for the first time, met these cousins. Our meeting on the program was brief, but afterwards I had lunch with three of my female cousins and felt a strange sensation to be chatting casually with relatives I never knew existed. My first cousin, Carol Battles, and I established a warm bond immediately, probably because we were both college teachers and she was completing her dissertation while raising a family, as I had done some years earlier. Plus, she had a great sense of humor about her newly discovered roots.

Our next in-family reunion occurred in October of 1993 in LaBrea, about an hour east of Los Angeles, where the Scott family had invited us to dinner. By another strange coincidence, Grace's only daughter, named Patricia like my youngest sister, had married Kenneth Scott. Their son Jeffrey had served as a link between the two families. My mother's mother had come from a large family of Scotts in Maryland, so it seemed fitting that a later generation of Scotts would bring the two sisters and their families back together again. A few months later Jeffrey Scott came up to spend a weekend with us on the Stanford campus. He and our younger son Lowell developed instant rapport and found they shared many mutual interests.

Within the next two years, Shirlee and I would enjoy visits with our two first cousins: Carol Battles and her family who own a Christmas tree farm in a suburb of Cleveland, Ohio, and Dottie Dunker, her children and grandchildren who live in the suburbs of Minneapolis. Dottie and Carol are half-sisters, the daughters of my mother's oldest brother, William Morris, who never informed his two wives about his black heritage. So we were eager to fill in the blanks about both sides of our Morris family tree. Our cousins' families were welcoming, gracious and as curious about us as we were about them. We discovered all kinds of amazing similarities, such as our first sons named Jeffrey (or Geoffrey) and our daughters named Margaret (or Peggy) or Patricia (or Patty). I couldn't help but wonder how many times our paths might have crossed with Dottie and her three children while we were living in Minneapolis in the early 1960s, when my husband was on the faculty of the University of Minnesota. Somehow the eerie coincidences that kept cropping up in our conversations with Carol and Dottie rekindled my fascination with the Jungian concept of the "collective unconscious" that links the minds and destinies of human beings.

Between these mini-reunions, I had spent the summer of 1993 in England as a Visiting Scholar at Birkbeck College at the University of London, where I was conducting research on Afro-Caribbean youth. After returning to my Kensington hotel one evening from a festive dinner with the only Black Lord and Black Lady in the British Empire, I received another momentous call from my sister, Shirlee. She excitedly blurted out, "Guess who we're related to—Judge Halyburton's mother was Martha "Patty" Dandridge, the favorite niece of Martha Washington. Cousin Hilda was right." Stunned and incredulous, I replied: "Do you mean *that* Martha Washington, George's wife? She laughed and said: "The same—her family name was Dandridge before she married Daniel Parke Custis, her first husband. Martha's brother Bartholomew named his eldest daughter after her."

I made some rapid mental calculations and exclaimed: "That means if Judge Halyburton was our Great-great Grandfather, then Martha Washington's brother was our Great-great-great grandfather, so we really are descended from the "First Families of Virginia." It took me a few minutes to absorb this news, which was just too amazing, but then I said, somewhat sarcastically: "We'll never be able to prove it without DNA or something more substantial than two old photographs." As the eternal optimist in the family, Shirlee said: "We'll see. Every day there's a new surprise and every clue yields another insight to our family lineage."

Motivated to learn more about the Dandridge connection, I donned my researcher's hat again and found a small library on the edge of London where colonial records were stored. During my final week in London, I took the Underground out to this charming suburb and began my search for the Dandridge family's English roots.

It turned out that they had been a prosperous, adventurous family, with one branch living on Fleet Street, the current center of the London publishing and media firms. Members of the Dandridge family emigrated from England to the colony of Virginia in the late seventeenth century, some as early as 1674, thus establishing the American branch of the Dandridge family long before the Revolutionary War.

The family prospered in the New World, producing statesmen, soldiers, gentlemen farmers, and successful entrepreneurs. Martha Dandridge and her brother were the children of Col. John Dandridge from New Kent County, Virginia, fated to become the father-in-law of the first president of the new nation. There is no way that Martha could have foreseen that her namesake's husband, the honorable Judge Halyburton, would unintentionally found a separate but unequal line of black descendants who would excel in their own right, without the benefits of royal patronage or racial privilege.

Before I left London at the end of that summer of 1993, I spent one Sunday afternoon browsing at the Portobello

Road Flea Market and came upon a stall selling crests of ancient British families. On a whim, I ordered custom-made wooden crests of the Halyburton clan, my Scottish forebears dating back to the eleventh century, for my two sisters and myself. I was astonished to discover that there was a head of a Moor at the top of the crest, above a knight's armored mask. In the meantime, Shirlee had found an illustration of the crest in a genealogy book and had chuckled at the Moor's curly Afro. The family motto "watch well" is displayed beneath a yellow and blue shield. Could it be that the Halyburton clan had an African ancestor who had drifted north after the Moorish invasion of Spain in the eighth century? Or was the Moor's head simply a symbol of a mythic warrior tradition in the Scottish highlands?

My quest to unravel the mystery of my Mother's missing Aunt Ruth took me next to Sao Paulo, Brazil. My husband and I were vacationing there in October of 1994 during the final stages of the World Cup soccer games. In 1916 my great aunt Ruth Morris had married John Tazewell Jones and moved to Sao Paulo a year later. After graduating from Harvard University in 1904 as the classmate of Franklin Delano Roosevelt, Jones had been unable to find a decent job as an engineer in America because of race. So the newly-weds decided to emigrate to Brazil where they could live their lives as fair-skinned blacks without the burden of racial discrimination. Ruth, like her two brothers, had opted to live her adult life in the white world, cutting her ties with virtually all of her past life, her family and friends.

From Jones' letters in his Class Reunion notes in the Harvard Archive, I found a Sao Paulo home address. With the help of the city librarian and the use of old city maps, we finally tracked it down. We took a taxi to the "American

Gardens" residential section where their home was located. Surprisingly we actually found the small colonial white adobe Catholic Church, shaded by a large palm tree. It was the site where Ruth had posed for a snapshot decades earlier, dressed in a fashionable gaucho-style hat, long skirt and stylish high top shoes.

After a brief visit to the church in an unsuccessful attempt to search their records for any evidence that the Jones were parishioners, Jim suggested that I duplicate the photo of my Aunt in that same spot as a souvenir of our visit. When we returned from South America, I sent a copy of this photo to my Mother and signed it, "With love from Sao Paulo, in memory of your Aunt Ruth."

However, the story of Aunt Ruth as an expatriate so far from home and family continued to haunt me. In 1992, the year we found Grace, my Mother's cousin Ruth, named after their Aunt, gave me permission to take a snapshot of her beautiful portrait hanging in their dining room in Washington. She told me that the portrait had once hung in the Chicago Art Institute.

In October 2002, when I was invited to Chicago to receive an award from the History Makers organization, I decided on an impulse to call the Art Institute to see if I could obtain any more information about the portrait. On my final morning in Chicago, I met with an archivist at the Institute who showed me several large catalogs of annual exhibits of Chicago-area artists at the Institute. After poring over several of these documents, I finally discovered an entry in 1917 of "Portrait of Ruth" by Charles Lesaar, a Belgian artist who priced the portrait at $1,000, a princely sum at that time. It was one of the most expensive in the exhibition. The stars must have been aligned perfectly for me that day. I learned from the museum's librarian that Mr. Lesaar had also lived in Oakland, California, where there were copies of his paintings in local collections, so that I might be able to compare the style of those paintings with the elegant lines and shadings of my Aunt Ruth's portrait in order to authenticate its provenance.

My search for my aunt Ruth had now come full circle, perhaps to be completed in my own backyard. When I left the museum, I paused on the broad steps a few moments to enjoy the view of the dynamic Chicago skyline. I smiled as I thought about the irony of my visit—one day after being honored as an African American woman achiever in the twenty-first century, I was reconstructing the past of a great-aunt whose portrait had hung as a "white" woman in one of the most prestigious museums in America, nearly a century earlier. I thought: "Hat's off to you, Aunt Ruth, you managed to have the last laugh about race in North *and* South America."

The odyssey in search of Aunt Grace and my Mother's family has taken me to libraries in six cities on three continents. But at some deeper level, I realize that there are some questions that can never be answered. We may empathize, from today's perspective, with their decision to live in the white world, but we will never fully understand how they felt about their lifelong deception and whether or not they experienced daily anxieties about being unmasked as black impostors.

Finding Aunt Grace has meant many things to me: the joy of reuniting my Mother with her only sister, the excitement of discovering a whole new extended family, and the satisfaction of uncovering the roots and branches of my Mother's fascinating family tree. While the emotional impact of these discoveries has lessened in the past decade, the intellectual impact continues to challenge me in many ways. Professionally, the story of my family's multiracial roots has probably enhanced my credibility as a scholarly authority on multiracial youth and their identity issues.

In recent years, the concept of "race" has become increasingly untenable scientifically, yet it remains an undeniable social reality that continues to shape our daily lives, our interactions, and our life options. When I look at the explosion of intermarriage and multiracial children in our society, I muse about their self-identities and how their visibility and viability will ultimately change the nature of American society.

With my own cafe au lait coloring, I have been mistaken for a creole in the Caribbean, a mulatto in Brazil, and a mestiza in Mexico: countries where centuries of racial mixture have produced beautiful multi-colored societies, bursting with the creativity and dynamism of hybrid vigor.

How will American society cope with its increasing racial and ethnic diversity? Will we develop into a stratified multiracial society like Brazil or South America? Or will we learn to live with the permutations of skin color and the ambiguities of racial identity?

My birth certificate identified me as "colored"; my family raised me as a "Negro"; I called myself "Black" in the civil rights movement of the 1960's; and became known as an "African American" in the 1990's. Through the evolution of all these racial labels, I was reared in a black family, nurtured by a black community and inspired by black role models and heroes who had triumphed over racism and oppression to achieve at least a piece of the American dream. Despite growing awareness of my multiracial roots,

I have always felt secure in my racial identity and comfortable in my brown skin.

In 2000 the U.S. Census for the first time allowed people to identify themselves with more than one racial or ethnic heritage, creating a "multiracial" category for analysis. When I finally found time to complete our household survey, in the midst of transition from college professor to retirement, I read all of the categories carefully. Without any hesitation or ambivalence, I firmly checked "African American."

JAMES LOWELL GIBBS

Jim is my mother's son-in-law, my brother-in-law, and my sister Jewelle's husband. He was born in the 1930s. Jim is the Martin Luther King, Jr., Centennial Professor of Anthropology Emeritus at Stanford University and editor of and contributor to Peoples of Africa *(1965) and coauthor of* Law in Radically Different Cultures *(1983).*

Shirlee's discovery of Mom's "long lost" family in 1992 had a dual impact for me. One was personal and familial. The other was professional and academic.

After thirty-six years of marriage to Jewelle, during which I became less and less of an "in-law," it was a jolt to be faced with a whole set of "new" family on her side. A "white" family at that. Even though we had known that they were "out there" somewhere, it was slightly unsettling to realize that I was going to actually meet them.

It was one thing for Jewelle's Aunt Grace and her family to meet my mother-in-law, who, after all, looked like them. How, I wondered, would they respond to me, the darkest member of the family?

I needn't have worried. The Sunday afternoon in 1993 when we crossed the threshold of the home of Ken Scott, Grace's son-in-law, he and his family could not have been more cordial. Ken, looking like a friendly teddy bear, set the tone, embracing each of us warmly. His three children and his son-in-law also were congenial.

Ken had a long-standing interest in American Indians and his home's decor included many Indian artifacts and paintings by Native American artists. So, in addition to the newly restored family ties, we each had an interest in "The Other," mine being rooted largely in my identity as an anthropologist.

Before the weekend was over, we learned of Jeff (Ken's son) Scott's interest in black music. Inviting us to his condominium, he proudly showed us his very large collection of CD's which had countless albums by black musicians, African American, African and African Diasporan.

Perhaps the most poignant event in the process of coming to know Jewelle's "white cousins" came at Christmas time that same year. Cousin Carol and her husband, Glen, a Christmas tree farmer in Ohio, flew out to San Francisco on Christmas Day to celebrate the holiday on the 26th, with Carol's daughter, Peggy, and her then husband, Jan Santos, a Filipino. We were invited to their "Christmas" dinner on the 26th.

Imagine our surprise when Peggy started dinner by lighting the first candle in a Kwanzaa kinara (candleholder). Carol announced: "In honor of our newly discovered heritage, we decided to celebrate Kwanzaa." Both of us were deeply touched—and slightly amused. While we had attended various Kwanzaa celebrations over the years since Kwanzaa had been established in 1966, we never had actually celebrated Kwanzaa in our own home. Successfully getting through all the various activities associated with Christmas was as much as our particular family dynamics could bear.

As a Kwanzaa gift, Carol's family gave us the *Kwanzaa Cookbook*. We did not dilute their pleasure by telling them that Shirlee and Harold had given us a copy a few years earlier.

We had feared that the "lost" white family would resent being "outed" by Shirlee's book, *The Sweeter the Juice*. But, *au contraire*, they took their "new" heritage in stride, embracing it as an enrichment. (But why shouldn't they? The Taylors, their "new" black family that "discovered" them were, after all, a family in which they could take pride—as I do.) The Scott family, which always had felt particularly small, since Ken and his late wife Patricia, Jewelle's first cousin, were only children, seemed especially glad to have found more "family."

The other impact on my life of the discovery of the "lost" family was professional. For many years I had taught a course entitled *Ethnographic Film* at Stanford University. In 1988 when I was appointed as the first holder of an endowed chair named after the Rev. Dr. Martin Luther King, Jr. I decided, in the spirit of the honor, to offer a new film course that would enlarge Stanford's curriculum in its Program in African and Afro American Studies.

The new course was entitled "Film Images of African American Culture" and it traced the cinematic treatment of African Americans and African American culture from 1915 when the notorious "Birth of a Nation" was released, forward to the present day. The course was an instant success with 1990s students who were quite visually oriented and visually experienced. As an added plus, the class consistently enrolled the highest proportion of African American students of any class I ever taught at Stanford—except for "Introduction to African and Afro-American Studies."

Combining the theme and historical thrust of my black film course with the theme of the role of race boundaries that animates Shirlee's book, I decided to write a paper that traced the treatment of the black/white race boundary in Hollywood feature films. I gave it the working title "Stone Wall to Picket Fence: Tracing the Race Boundary in American Film." The paper notes that in 1915, *Birth of a Nation*'s take on the race boundary was that it was a stone wall to be breached only with dire consequences for the boundary crossers. Later films like the original *Imitation of Life* and *Pinky* reflected the same view.

Films of subsequent decades portrayed some fence hopping: from the black side to the white side in *Guess Who's Coming to Dinner* or *Watermelon Man;* and from the white side to the black side in *True Identity*. Other boundary-related films focus on the dilemma of the bi-racial child, e.g., *Carbon Copy;* of the buddy film in which one buddy is white and the other is black, e.g., *Beverly Hills Cop.* In these films, the fence shifts from stone wall to a picket fence, the barrier is more permeable. More recently, *Monster's Ball* suggests that the fence, the boundary, has almost disappeared. So, the working title of my paper may need recasting.

The discovery of the Morris missing relatives heightened my interest in the black/white racial boundary, the one with which most Americans are most obsessed and increased my insight into its tangible professional outcome stimulated by Shirlee's "discovery."

HAROLD CORNELIUS HAIZLIP

Harold Haizlip is my husband of forty-five years. As an educator with an Ed.D. from Harvard, he has been a teacher, a private school headmaster, the commissioner of education for the U.S. Virgin

Islands, a college vice president, a corporate executive, and a non-profit foundation director. Harold was born in the 1930s.

"Oh my God!" I thought, standing in the foyer of the Taylor home for the first time in the early afternoon on Thanksgiving Day, 1957. "Shirlee's mother is white! I'll be damned!"

Her hand outstretched toward me, Mrs. Taylor had just emerged, smiling broadly, from stashing "Dutchess," her German Shepherd, in the kitchen so that I could meet the family for the first time without being attacked. Dutchess ignored the family members who had gathered, but I was a newcomer. As the family guardian, she had a job to do and therefore continued barking loudly, straining to free herself from the choke chain anchored to a kitchen door knob. "God help me if she ever gets loose," I thought. Very attractive, well-dressed and gracious, Mrs. Taylor welcomed me warmly and encouraged Shirlee to introduce me to Reverend Taylor and the family and show me to the Guest Room while she and Dutchess took care of the last-minute dinner preparations.

Mrs. Taylor's warmth and gentility became quite evident as she inquired about my family, my growing up in Washington, D.C., and my graduating from her beloved alma mater, Dunbar High School, where several of my favorite teachers were friends of hers. We had many other "connections" across D.C.'s landscape. She was intrigued that I had majored in Latin and Greek. I liked her. We bonded on many different levels. And regardless of her appearance, I realized she was a black woman through and through.

During the years that followed, slowly but surely I learned about Mom's abandonment by her family as a young child and began to understand that in her proactive love for, and support of, her husband, her children, her foster daughters and her grandchildren, she was providing the constancy, affection, and safe haven that as a child she, herself, had been denied—perhaps living through them the childhood she never had. She often became melancholy or feisty when she talked about the father and siblings who vanished and never returned to claim her, proud that she had nevertheless survived. I could feel, however, that the hurt was still there, deep down within her soul.

In the early '90s when Shirlee decided to intensify her efforts to solve the mystery of Mom's family, I was eager to help. I thought that the most we could expect was to find out when Mom's siblings died and where they were buried. I hoped this information would give Mom some measure of closure, of relief—and perhaps even release—from her life-long pain as an unwitting orphan.

Shirlee's mission to close Mom's family circle did more than reunite two sisters who had lived apart on different sides of the color line for more than 76 years. It also brought together black and white members of the same family who had no prior knowledge of each others' existence, and provided for everyone a previously unknown history of the family's origins extending back to the Founding Fathers of the United States. In so doing, the family's story further became a discourse on race and identity, on the pain of racism and family secrets past and present, and on our struggles to be free and find happiness in our lives.

After growing up in segregated Washington, D.C., and attending segregated, all-Negro schools prior to the launch of the civil rights movement, I received academic scholarships to attend Amherst College and Harvard University, two of the Ivy League's most prestigious institutions. Class, caste and hostility toward racial differences were my constant companions. Yet even as the civil rights marches and conflagrations escalated, I found myself making lifelong friends across the great divides of race, class and cultural history, because of shared interests, hopes and dreams. Despite the entrenched opposition, I became an integrationist who dreamed of a world not divided by race or ethnic differences. I continue to be an integrationist these many years later.

As it unfolded, Mom's story became mindboggling for me because it demonstrated beyond question that the integration I sought in my own life and encouraged others to aspire to was academic, if not irrelevant: despite differences in our ethnicity, our physical appearances and our life circumstances, we're all related! If as a society we could accept this fact, we all could become ". . . free, at last." Mom's and Shirlee's white family reached out to us with open arms, readily acknowledging a common heritage and eager to become acquainted as family. I am still processing the ultimate meaning of this stunning development—for me, personally, for us as a family, and for American society as a whole. Our story is not unique. It is commonplace. It is our shared history.

Mom's history crashed down on me in another very personal way, quite unexpectedly. The photos we obtained of Mom's never-before-seen progenitors, parents and siblings dredged up from the deep recesses of my childhood memories a photograph of my maternal grandfather. My grandmother prominently displayed it in the living room of her house deep in the back woods of Kernersville, North Carolina, where as a child I spent every summer—without electricity, central heat, indoor toilets, or running water. Because my grandfather had died before I was born, I never met him. But decades later, Shirlee's research for *The*

Sweeter the Juice reminded me of that photograph of him. He was different, I recalled. Very pale. Straight hair. White looking. I had never thought to ask, so out of the blue I telephoned my mother and blurted out, "Was your father white?"

"Of course he was!" she said. "Don't start no mess, now. He's dead and gone. Resting in peace."

Ever since this latter-day revelation, yet another confirmation of Mom's story, I have become even more convinced that we are all interconnected across the barriers that appear to divide us, and that race is a social construct, more so than a scientific or biological reality.

What began as Shirlee's search for her Mom's family has turned out to be the greatest gift we can offer each other: the brotherhood of mankind.

CAROL MORRIS BATTLES

Carol Morris Battles was born in the 1940s. She is the younger daughter of my mother's brother Bill Morris. Because each girl had a different mother, the two half sisters had never met until my family explorations brought them together. That coming together pleases everyone. Carol had no knowledge of her family's black heritage until I called her in 1992. Carol lives now with her husband in Ohio. When I first met her, she was working on her Ph.D., which she has since acquired.

The Sweeter the Juice has not impacted my lifestyle, my career, or my relationships with close family and friends, however it has had a large influence on how I think about prejudice and racism. I have chosen to use this event as a pivotal point from which to learn and to grow. I could have swept it under the carpet and remained forever White. However I decided to embark on a journey to find out what it is like to be Black in

America today. That was not an easy task since my looks
didn't change and I did not darken my skin with chemicals.

I work for a Community College that has a mission
involving diversity acceptance and tolerance for all, so it
provided for a comfortable environment from which to
learn about racial issues. My colleagues thought my change
in racial status was a good thing in that we now had more
diversity in the faculty ranks. I also belong to a church that
practices radical inclusivity. This provided for an opportunity to engage in interesting diversity discussions.

At the time the story broke I was a doctoral student
preparing for oral comprehensive exams with the plan to do
my research on elderly women and nutrition. That plan
quickly changed as I decided to investigate racial issues in
America, instead. I had no idea what an overwhelming task
that would be and no idea what it was like to experience prejudice first hand. I soon discovered that racism is alive and well
and living in America and that prejudice is a perceived reality.

The story for me really began with the *Oprah* show.
When the story aired, I was a little apprehensive about how
it would be received. I had made the decision to go public
with the fact that I was not really White after all. At forty-
plus years, I was a little old for an identity crisis but I was
still a little unsure of the reaction I would get. Having a
Black family was all pretty new and of course I hadn't had
the time or capability to tell everyone.

I didn't need to worry because there was literally no
reaction. Millions of people watched that show and yet that
evening no one called except one good friend and my own
children. I knew friends and neighbors had watched. I had
told enough people plus the television promotions had featured me. Yet no one called. I was dismayed until my hus-

band figured it out. Carol, he said, they simply don't know what to say.

We are taught to say congratulations at appropriate times. We know how to extend condolences after a tragedy but we are simply not prepared to react when someone suddenly changes their racial classification. They did not know if this was good or bad. What should one say? Better to say nothing. When I saw people they either did not acknowledge the issue at all or they said I "looked nice."

One of the first things I noticed when I began telling the story to first time listeners was that they often, but not always, changed their physical distance based on their race. Blacks almost always moved closer to me frequently touching or hugging me. A Black woman actually grabbed me and yelled with delight in a crowded auditorium, "You're one of us."

The white reaction is quite different. Many Whites but certainly not all, lean back, step back, or move as far away as they can given the space we are in. They look pensively at me and are not too sure what to make of the whole thing. Outside of my safe world of academia or my church the reactions are not kind. Behind my back people say things like "that's too bad" or "how unfortunate." To my face I've gotten such responses as "I can't believe you are dealing so well with this tragedy," or "why would you air your dirty laundry in public?" When I point out the fact that they are proud of being German I get a blank look and a response like "that's different, you're talking about a different race." My observations support what the research literature has found and that is racism is still a pervasive part of American society. It is no longer overt but it is ever present and very covert. Usually Whites have no idea they have negative racial attitudes, truly believing themselves not [to] be prejudiced against Blacks.

I have also learned that to some extent everyone harbors some prejudice; that is, we prejudge people based on faulty and inflexible generalizations. An example of this involves my prior knowledge of the overt racism verbalized by some acquaintances of ethnic heritage. They have a seasonal party at a time when I am usually out of town attending an annual professional meeting. My husband has frequently attended solo. They were discussing this upcoming event at a gathering and inquiring if I would be available this time. As it was I was not going to be away and said that I would love to attend. I was looking forward to some great ethnic food. The matter was settled except for the actual date.

I was waiting for the invitation before making other social commitments and getting perplexed when I realized that after our conversation the story of my racial heritage had broken. They were racists. I was Black. I was not going to ever be invited to their house. I was angry. Driving by their house I gave it very nasty looks. Then I was hurt, then back to angry. I was the victim, the outsider, and the unwelcome one. They were the evil racists. How embarrassing to find out that something had happened in their family and the event never took place that year. I had prejudged them based on faulty generalizations. I was expressing prejudice; they were the innocents.

I also learned on other occasions that the differences between perceived racial discrimination and actual racial discrimination are difficult to discern. There is a changing nature to racism that has evolved from the civil rights era in the 1960s. It is modern racism. Whites may reject the concept of racism in principle but may react negatively if efforts towards equality infringe on their economic or social freedoms or change the racial status quo.

Integration is acceptable until it affects meaningful areas

of one's life. I witnessed this with a cousin on my mother's side. He is a proud card carrying member of the KKK and possibly a grand dragon of some sort. He has long been verbally overt in his expression of negative racial attitudes and has a history of getting into many physical fights in the past. He is now faced with the fact that "those people" are working with him. He thinks that some of "them" are okay. He has eaten a meal with a few, but they are the "good ones."

My father was his favorite uncle. They were very close and spent a lot of time together. I watched as he went through the stages of grief when I told him that his favorite uncle was half Black. He denied it was true, he was angry with "those people" for lying to me, he denied and he bargained. I don't know if resolution has yet arrived. He accepted integration of his work place but integration of his family is not yet acceptable.

While racism still exists in America, studies indicate that it is moving in a positive, less prejudiced direction. I had always tried to model racial acceptance for my children, never suspecting that "they were us." Encouraging them to invite black schoolmates to our home (difficult to do when there was maybe one or two Black families in the whole community). I bought my daughter a Black doll when most Black kids didn't have them because there were no Black girls in her class. Oddly I never suspected that we had Black heritage even though there were lots of indicators that I totally missed. It truly never occurred to me.

I harbor no anger towards my father for passing and not telling me. He had learned as a child that Black was not a good thing and that the only way to be able to live and support a family was as White. I harbor only sadness that a wonderful, bright, loving black family was absent from my life all those years. Some passed away and I never got to meet them. My Aunt Margaret I only met a few times. I wish she could have been my "auntie" when I was growing up.

I do get angry when people say I couldn't know what it is like to be black because I haven't suffered the evils of racism. Racism divided my family. Racism kept us apart during our formative years. Racism ripped the souls of our very foundation. Racism forced those that could pass to leave behind their heritage and go into the world with less than a sixth grade education and fend for themselves.

Racism is the belief that race accounts for differences in human character or ability and that a particular race is superior to others. I am here to tell you that race does not make some one superior or inferior. The individual decides who and what they will become, not their heritage or their race. We are in control of our destiny; we need to accept responsibility for what we have become. Our heritage provides the framework, wheels, color and motor. We are the drivers of our destiny.

DONNA DUNKER DUMMER

Donna Dummer is the daughter of Dorothy Morris Dunker. Donna is my mother's grandniece and my first cousin once removed. She is a retired high school administrator. Donna was born in the 1940s.

Hi Shirlee . . .

I would like to share some thoughts that stay in my mind as I think about your book, *The Sweeter the Juice.* I'm encouraging my mother to write to you. Glen retired from Red Wing Shoe Company after thirty-two years of traveling internationally. I just retired from Red Wing High School as the student activities coordinator. We especially love traveling to see our children and grandchildren and spending time at the cabin in northern Wisconsin.

The whole concept of realizing there was more to my family background than I ever expected was unbelievable, but also exciting!!

Sometimes I still shake my head in awe how Shirlee was able to do all the research, write a book, and even have some family members meet for the first time. One of which is my mother, Dorothy Morris Dunker and her half sister, Carol Morris Battles. Since their initial meeting, they have had many chances to talk on the phone and visit each other. I also reflect on the fact Shirlee was able to reunite her mother, Margaret, and her sister Grace. My heart goes out to sweet Margaret as I imagine what it must have been like to be without family for so many years.

Even though my few minutes of fame on the *Oprah* show was a memorable experience, the local public reaction of our family story still lingers. Every year the psychology teacher at Red Wing High School replays the tape for his class when they study human relations. I worked at the high school for years, so each year many students would let me know they had "just" seen me on Oprah.

As our families continue to grow, I would hope someday we could meet even more of the Morris Clan . . . maybe a reunion is in order?!

Good luck in your new venture and a BIG hello to Harold.

Donna

BARBARA DUNKER HOFFMAN
Barbara Dunker Hoffman is the sister of Donna Dunker Dummer. She is the daughter of Dorothy Morris Dunker. She is my mother's grand-niece and my first cousin once removed. She lives in Bloomington, Minnesota, with her husband and family. Ebullient and

cheerful, Barbara has been a font of information about her family and their doings. Her annual Christmas letters are full of exuberant reports of the family's comings and goings of the previous year. Barbara currently works in an insurance broker/risk management company. Barbara was born in the 1950s.

Hi Shirlee . . .

Hope you had a great Thanksgiving with your family. There were almost 30 of us at my Mom's and Ollie's apartment party room. Lots of food and talk and laughs. How did you celebrate the big day? Les, the boys and I attended a wedding reception yesterday for our friends —he is Vietnamese and she is a tall, blond American. They are a very nice looking couple who showed us a great time and elegant Vietnamese dinner with shrimp, squid, quail, lobster, etc. etc. Had fun tasting new foods (to us anyway!) and trying to guess what they were saying in their native tongue. Yes, the world is filled with so many kinds and colors of people.

As a result of Shirlee's *The Sweeter the Juice,* my life has become more full and my family has increased in numbers. I did not know many things about my ancestors until I talked with Shirlee and read her book about our family. I was not aware that my grandfather, William Morris, Jr. (my mother's father), was black and moved to Ohio to "become" a white person to find a job. As a fair-skinned white person, when I first tell people that I'm part black, they look at me with questioning eyes, saying, "But you're so pale!"

I've been proud to show off the pictures of my newfound aunts, uncles and cousins. I'm proud that Shirlee and Jewelle and their families are doing well, travel frequently and have written books. It was fun to see my sister Donna meet the "other half" of the family on the Oprah Winfrey television show. And it was exciting to be asked to be on *Oprah* the following year, but disappointing when the producers changed the plan of the show and told me the night before that they were changing the show's format and would not need my brother Steve and me. It was great to see my niece Darcy on another TV talk show and to have Donna become well known in Red Wing, Minnesota because she was on the *Oprah* show.

The first time we met Shirlee was when she visited St. Paul, Minnesota on one of her book tours. She came to the Hungry Mind Bookstore to discuss her recently published *The Sweeter the Juice.* By the time my mother, brother and my children arrived at the bookstore, the discussion had already started and there were no chairs to sit. We stood at the back of the room admiring Shirlee and intently listening to her tales. When one member of the audience asked her if she had met all of her white family yet, Shirlee said, "Well, I am meeting some of them tonight for the first time and they are standing in the back of the room." All eyes turned around to look at us as we humbly smiled and waved to her, while holding our copies of *The Sweeter the Juice,* which we wanted Shirlee to autograph. After the book discussion the audience filed out, looking at us from head to toe. We chuckled afterwards, describing how we felt like animals in the zoo.

We then went to Shirlee's hotel and thoroughly enjoyed getting to know her. It was a wonderful evening, meeting Shirlee and talking with her like we had known her for years.

Shirlee's book taught me so much about my family. I'm pleased to tell people about my heritage, which I learned from the book. It's a very interesting book of history. I enjoy telling people I am related to the first President George Washington. I feel like I can associate with the slaves and what they went through because some of them were my blood relatives. I feel bad when I hear about the Indians getting free land and not having to pay taxes, yet the black people who must have suffered unspeakable indignities on their way up from slavery are still struggling.

It was interesting to learn about my grandfather who always wore hats and long sleeved shirts even in the summertime so his skin wouldn't get any darker. My grandmother, his first wife, has passed away now; I wonder what she would have thought if she knew she had married a black man. I have a small wooden box my grandmother gave to me that was my grandfather's. It is even more special to me now.

Since the book was published we have also met and spent time with my mom's half-sister Carol and her husband Glen and son Adam. It's fun for me to see my mom enjoy having a sister, as she was brought up as an only child. Carol is thrilled that we call her our aunt, because she was brought up as an only child also. More family members means more love to go around.

Shirlee, Jewelle, Aunt Margaret and their families have opened their hearts and arms to us, their newly found white cousins. I'm appreciative of the time and research that went into the creation of *The Sweeter the Juice.* Growing up, I never felt superior to people with different colored skin from me. They still had the same "insides." I knew the world was made up of all colors of people; I just didn't know our family had so many beautiful shades.

Love you lots,
Cousin Barb

DEIRDRE TAYLOR HAIZLIP

Deirdre is the older daughter of Harold and me. She is my mother's granddaughter. She was born in the 1960s and graduated from Yale University and Fordham Law School. She lives in the San Francisco area. Deirdre helped me with some of my initial research for The Sweeter the Juice.

For years, talk about my mother's family's multi-ethnic heritage was nothing more than white noise for me. I was Soul Sister Number One. As a pre-teen I wore Afro puffs and sat in the sun to get the darkest tan possible. As a teenager I sat under the dryer in curlers for hours to achieve a coveted Afro. For me, there was never a question about which side of the color line I claimed.

Finding Grace and her family made me face a part of my being that I had not acknowledged and that had not acknowledged me—the white side. The reunion changed many of my perceptions—about race, our family and the unshared history that followed the sisters' separation. It was a time to forgive, to reach out across the color lines as we knew them and embrace our long lost family members.

Jeff and I immediately bonded through our eclectic musical tastes and our love of nightlife. In Grace I recognized both my grandmother's fondness for animals and her quiet strength. My biggest fear—rejection by the other "white" family members—was unfounded. Everyone was genuinely anxious to meet and acknowledge us.

Once the dust settled I re-examined my definitions of race. What, beyond physical attributes and other external cues makes one black or white? Why would anyone deny any part of themself? If Nana was too black to be accepted, then I must be, too.

As Grace's story unfolded, I was able to release my anger about Nana's abandonment. The events following the reunion closed the loop for Nana. She found her birth sister and her other blood relatives. She embraced, enjoyed and forgave, paving the way for all of us to do the same.

In the past ten years my acceptance of the newer family members has led me to be more open to the fluidity of race. Most importantly I have realized that my status as Soul Sister Number One is not diminished by my other heritage. I proudly give new meaning to the term "Black Irish"!

MELISSA MORRIS HAIZLIP

Melissa is the younger daughter of Harold and me. She is my mother's granddaughter. She was born in the 1960s and went to Yale University. She lives in Los Angeles and is an actress and dancer. Melissa assisted in reading various drafts of The Sweeter the Juice.

"That Melissa, she's full of the Dickens!" These are the words of my great Aunt Grace, whose re-entry into the branches of our family tree changed the lives of many.

In addition to having a profound effect on our family, the story behind *The Sweeter the Juice* has impacted a huge spectrum of lives. As one of the daughters of the author, I've had numerous encounters with people of all races, with whom the book has resonated deeply. Almost ten years later, there remains a high level of interest in the story. Recently, at a cocktail party in Beverly Hills, California, folks were mesmerized by the cinematic arc of the story. In a bookstore in Larchmont Village in Los Angeles, once the owners realized I was related to one of their favorite authors, they marveled animatedly at the family history. Even in New York City, where I lived for over fifteen years, my black, white, Jewish, and multi-racial friends were all intrigued. Mostly, when people hear my last name, they ask me if I'm related to "that woman who wrote the book" or "those people on *Oprah*." I've become an unofficial ambassador of the book.

It's hard to fathom how many lives, young and old, this story has touched. For many, it continues to fascinate, educate and entertain, while illuminating the whole notion of identity and the conundrum of race in our country.

When my mother first found Grace, it was both exhilarating and daunting. We knew we'd been looking for the lost side of the family, but we never thought they'd be looking for us. Getting to know everyone proved to be gratifying and rewarding. As we spent holidays together and exchanged letters, I learned about the personalities and histories of my "new" relatives. What resulted from this great reunion was a sense of healing. I couldn't help thinking how lucky I was to be alive to witness a huge break in the family circle being restored. I knew that without my mother's arduous journey to find Grace, we would have missed out on an opportunity for closure on a grand karmic scale. Meeting our newly-found relatives for the first time was reversing, in a way, the damage of four generations of rejection, abandonment, and deceit. How often does one get to experience *that* turn of events in a lifetime? I felt, and still feel, lucky.

My cousin Jeff Scott and I became very close. We shared anthropology books like the Mayan book of creation, and world music by the Sufi devotional singer Nusrat Fateh Ali Khan. Jeff saw me perform on Broadway in

Jelly's Last Jam and in Randy Newman's *Faust* at the La Jolla Playhouse. When I had a summer house in the Hamptons, he came to visit. Over time we've discussed what we knew immediately upon meeting; a brief harmonic convergence which would reveal we had more in common than our differences.

The Sweeter the Juice, provocative in nature, has sparked many a debate on the theory of identity. I find it interesting to think about identity from one generation to the next. What's remarkable is the difference between the past and the present: how a race has been outwardly defined by color, and how people choose to define themselves today. The older generations have made the choice, whether personally or due to life's circumstances, to define themselves outwardly, by their socio-economic, educational, and personal achievements both at home and in their chosen professional fields. In contrast, as a child appearing after the Civil Rights movement and growing up in the twenty-first century, my identity has been defined more by personal and spiritual growth from within. Since the road has already been paved, I have searched to find meaning, a sense of place, existence and peace. A life informed by equality has led me to be open, patient and understanding. I see myself as an "inclusionist," lacking racist or separatist ideals. I believe the story of our family has helped others to re-examine their views on race and identity in America. After all, we are not always who we think we are, nor who we appear to be. I do not think that a stranger glancing at me walking down the street would expect me—an otherwise average African American woman—to be related to the first lady of our country, Martha Washington. Therein lies the American paradox—the result of choices made long ago.

Finding the "new" family has allowed us to come full circle. In a letter written March 3, 1994, my Aunt Grace wrote:

> Dear Melissa:
> Thank you for the lovely Valentine card. So dear of you to remember me. I will always have a special place in my heart for you.

I was moved by her ability to embrace me, her black sister's granddaughter, after well over seventy-six years. I imagine that one day my grandmother Nana and her sister, Grace, will walk hand in hand in heaven, where there is no color line. I'd like to think that in the end, we still choose love.

DARCY MICCIO PACE

Darcy Pace was born in the 1960s. She recently acquired a Ph.D. in nursing and works as a district nurse for a public school system in Colorado. She has one four-year-old son and remarried in June of 2003. She grew up in Minnesota and is the daughter of Donna Dummer. She is my mother's grand-niece. I first met her when she was living and working in San Diego.

Shirlee,
I have had only positive experiences, with the exception of one individual in the very beginning, regarding the news of my family. My Caucasian friends had comments like, "wow," "were you shocked?" "I'm not surprised." One African American coworker approached me only 2 weeks ago and asked, "Darcy, I don't mean to offend you, but do you have any black blood in you?" So, of course, I told her the story.

One close friend that I grew up with, who happens to be mixed, was also not surprised. When I told her the news, she just smiled and said she always knew. We used to have tanning contests as teenagers, and half of the time, I was darker than she was.

I feel blessed to have had the opportunity to meet a few members of my new family. I was fortunate enough to be chosen to appear on the Fox TV newsmagazine show *Front Page*. I was flown to Los Angeles where I was taken to Shirlee and Harold's home to meet them, Jeff Scott and my Aunt Margaret. It was a dramatic introduction due to the television taping, but such an incredible moment that has made great memories for me. This is a group of intelligent, beautiful people with warm and loving hearts, and I'm so proud to call them my family.

Love, Darcy

JEFFREY TAYLOR AND JULIE TAYLOR-MASSEY

Jeffrey and Julie are brother and sister. They are the children of my brother, Julian. Their mother is Irish. Jeff is completing his master's degree in civil engineering at Tufts University. He has worked on the Big Dig in Boston, among other projects. Julie holds an M.B.A. and is working toward a Ph.D. in developmental psychology. They were both born in the 1970s and spent a good part of their childhood with their Irish grandparents in a small town close to Boston.

The story of our family touched us deeply. It has served as a reminder to embrace our family, culture, and history, all of which can be sometimes taken for granted. Furthermore, it has taught us that being aware of the past, in particular our ancestors and their lives, helps us reflect on the type of lives we live today, want to live in the future, and want to provide for the next generation of Taylors—lives that are filled with love, equality, forgiveness, tolerance, and most importantly, family.

KEVIN HOFFMAN

Kevin Hoffman is the son of Barbara Dunker Hoffman and Les Hoffman. Kevin was born in the 1980s and is a recent graduate of Carlson School of Management at the University of Minnesota. He is my mother Margaret's grand-nephew.

The first thing that comes to mind when I'm given the opportunity to explain our unusual family history tends to be the same anecdote. I've chosen to use this story, which amuses most people, to begin my thoughts on how this discovery has changed my life. I thought it was so cool to learn that I actually had a very interesting and exciting family history.

I usually begin my tale by explaining how we met Shirlee and Harold, Jewelle and Jim and how we also had the opportunity to meet our relatives in Ohio, the Battleses. However, the most interesting part of my experience, I explain, took place in my eighth grade English class. We had just finished up a lesson on multi-culturalism and were about to begin a new topic. My teacher, Mrs. Beagle, usually sat at the front of the class for the first few minutes to talk about local news and open the day on a less scholarly note.

However, on this particular day, she had the TV/VCR rack pulled to the front of the room. She wanted to talk once more about the amazing diversity the United States has. She then explained how she saw this wonderful talk show about an interesting story regarding a family's history with race.

As soon as she said this, I became quite positive she was going to show the *Oprah* episode featuring the reunion of our family's "two sides." Sure enough, the tape started and we watched a good portion of the reunion episode. The whole time it played, I thought to myself what an odd coincidence it was that I had just happened to bring *The Sweeter the Juice* with me to school that day. Mrs. Beagle turned the machine off and raved that it was such an interesting tale of race in America. She went on, as she usually did, to see if anyone had any thoughts on the subject.

I slowly raised my hand (at this time I was hardly a good public speaker) and said, "Yea, that was my aunt on *Oprah*, and that story was about my family." Astonished, she asked if I happened to have the book with me, and if I'd come up and tell a little about what had happened. So I slowly went up to the front of the class and explained the whole story, from discovery to the present.

Most people had a hard time believing it, but the family tree and most importantly *Oprah*, really helped back up my story. We spent the rest of the afternoon just talking about the different implications and feelings I had and would face in the future.

To this day, some people still laugh and do not believe me. This is most likely due to the incredibly pale skin I possess, but I don't let it bother me. I take a lot of pride in knowing who I really am, and where I came from. I've also used this story in my college communication classes to introduce myself. I still see some people who disbelieve, but for the most part, people think it's very interesting and fascinating to hear about.

Although I can't say that finding this out has had a major impact on my life, it has, however, made me realize that our society is more diverse than ever and will continue to grow in that direction. It will become rare to have a "pure" racial or ethnic background. In a sense, I feel America is already this way. Some people just don't know, investigate or sadly care enough about their origins to take the time to find out. I was once this way, but I can now feel special in that I know from who and where my family has grown and expanded.

PART III

The Color of Letters

PHOTOGRAPH ON PREVIOUS PAGE IS OF
MARGARET MORRIS TAYLOR, CIRCA 1957

16

Open Hearts, Open Minds

As soon as the book was published, the letters began to come. Letters from professionals, blue-collar workers, no-collar workers, housewives, ministers, students, adoptees, and mixed-race people. From the North, South, East, and West. Words flew across the water from Australia and Hawaii. Hearts opened. Sepia-toned pictures tumbled from envelopes. Even hair samples found their way to my desk for my inexpert review. Each letter had its own story.

And still they come. They make me laugh. They make me cry. They make me think. Most of all, I cherish the idea that people take time to sit down and write to a stranger about her family's life story. That moves me deeply. I answer every letter. What follows is a selection. The rest could fill two books.

Unexpected Treasures

Dear Mrs. Haizlip:

I purchased your book after I saw you discussing it on the Oprah Winfrey show. I glanced up while working around the house and became extremely interested when I recognized a picture of one of your ancestors. James Dandridge Halyburton is my husband's great-great grandfather.

My mother-in-law has become the Suits family genealogist and I have enclosed information from her Halyburton family writings about Peyton Gwynn Halyburton (my husband's great grandfather), Edward Everett Morris' half brother. I hope that you find them as interesting as I do.

After looking up the Halyburton family and finding several photographs, I was struck by Peyton and Edward's resemblance. My husband's brother Peyton also shows his Halyburton ancestry and looks a bit like his great grandfather Peyton.

As you can see from Peyton's short biography, both Edward and Peyton lived in Washington, D.C., at the same time and I wonder if they knew of each other's existence. They were so close in age, I would like to know what their relationship was like while they were living with their father in Richmond. Were they close? I have so many questions that will probably never be answered.

I truly enjoyed your book and am glad that I have found another part of the family. Should you care to correspond with us, we would be delighted.

Sincerely,
Linda Norbut Suits, Illinois

(Author's note: The Haizlips met the Suits on a follow-up *Oprah* show. They exchange correspondence and Christmas cards. Each promises to visit the other.)

Dear Shirlee:

I too have been meaning to write, but since we have been getting so much "help" doing everything from changing the oil in the car, to pruning trees to writing letters, you can probably guess why I haven't yet.

In the madness after the taping, one of the guests approached me near the entrance. . . . He said, "Your reaction seemed a bit reserved. How did you really feel? Didn't you feel a bit diminished?" The more I think about that question, the more angry I get. First of all, my reaction was genuine, and if it seemed reserved, it was because I am reserved by nature.

Secondly, the assumption that I should have felt diminished when I found out I have black cousins was even more upsetting. I thought the whole point of the show was to judge a person on his or her character, and not the color of his skin, or his relative's skin either. I would think anyone should be proud to find out they have intelligent, articulate, upstanding cousins regardless of color.

It promises to be a busy and rapidly approaching spring. I have my herbs started indoors for the garden, and plans for the vegetable garden that will get started in April. As Linda has already mentioned, the baby is scheduled for arrival in April, and the lawn will spring to life about then too.

Well, we have to take Kathryn to the doctor this morning to see about those ears of hers. Stay in touch, and I will do the same.

Dustin Suits, Illinois

(Author's note: Dustin Suits is the husband of Linda Suits and the author's cousin through the Halyburton line.)

Dear Shirlee—

We're so excited to find more "family"—I'm glad you decided to do research about our family history. We are so proud of you and your family and the book you wrote. Congratulations. . . . I hope sometime soon we can meet you. My sister Donna was pleased to be on Oprah's show and to meet you. She was sorry she couldn't spend more time with you and your family (oops—we're all family!)

To explain who I am—I am Dorothy's daughter . . . married for twenty-three years to Les Hoffman. He is the Operations Manager of the Lock Division for Floyd Security—he manages 20 plus locksmiths, 4 retail stores that sell safes, locks, etc. and the inventory for everything. I work for an advertising agency—I worked there for four years—then we were transferred to Chicago for four years and were transferred back to Minnesota. Then I went back to work at the advertising agency—and I have been there since.

Les and I have three children—Jeff, eighteen years, is a senior at high school plays baseball and basketball. Kevin is 14 years old and in eighth grade. He plays baseball, basketball and soccer and hockey. Trisha is seven years old and in second grade. She is a Brownie Girl Scout. (I am one of her leaders.) Tomorrow we will be talking about women in history—and we will talk about the book you wrote! Perfect timing! She also takes tap, ballet and jazz.

I keep busy teaching Sunday school, working on Jeff's graduation party in June and attending the kids' games. We have 4 basketball games a week and during baseball season we usually have a game or two every night. I'm sewing a cheerleading outfit for Trisha now because she "cheers" with the high school varsity cheerleaders at Jeff's basketball games. Take care—say hello to your family,

> Love
>
> Barb [Barbara Dunker Hoffman], Minnesota

Shirlee:

I've just finished reading your book, it was well done.

It was riveting; it evoked great empathy for your mother, Margaret.

I felt her pain, her hurt, her rage, her loneliness, and strangely her guilt of what did I do that made my family abandon me. What a burden to have to carry that kind of emptiness.

In spite of the wonderful feeling of finding a lost sister and a further extension of family, it's unfortunate that this story has not been brought to fruition.

The many questions raised in my mind are what kind of cold and unfeeling people are the father and other siblings who could abandon a small child and for all intent denied her existence, appalling behavior and inexcusable.

I found Margaret was a warm, gracious and loving person and deserves all the love and attention you and the rest of the family give her. I wish her happiness and good health.

Please forgive the scribble as I'm writing this at work between the crush of business and I wanted to convey my emotions and immediate first impressions.

I hope you are glowing in a sense of pride for having brought these sisters together and bringing this saga to the extended family and to the rest of the public.

With warmest regards,

Ken Scott, California

(Author's note: Ken Scott is the widower of my first cousin Patricia Cramer Scott, my aunt Grace's only daughter. Ken is Grace's son-in-law and the father of three children, my first cousins once removed, Jeffrey, Laura, and Lisa. Ken has since died.)

Dear Shirlee,

I feel I can address you by your first name because I am a childhood friend of Dorothy Morris Dunker. We had not spoken for almost sixty years—until she called to tell me about her "news." She wanted to share it with me because I was her only friend "who went back that far." (I hasten to explain that we had exchanged Christmas cards and family news during that time.)

I have you to thank for that call—for we were immediately on a "sister" basis despite the years gone by.

Our families were friends and we spent a great deal of time together. Upon reflection, I could remember my mother observing that Grace Cramer was always putting on white powder and saying "the frizzy hair" will always "out." Being a pre-teenager it all went over my head. I just knew Bertha and Billy—Grace and Earl as family friends and accepted them as such—and Dotty and I enjoyed an almost sister relationship. In our mid teens our paths parted tho I remember hearing that Bill had left his family. By then I had moved to Warren, Ohio to pursue life after graduation.

Having such a close interest I immediately ordered your book and devoured it 2–3 times . . .

I fell in love with "Aunt Margaret" and my heart bleeds for her years of separation and deprivation. Maybe the trials and tribulations account for her sweetness of spirit which is almost ethereal. Did she turn to God for the Grace to see her thru?

I thank you all from the bottom of my heart for the dedication and years of work which resulted in this book and enabled the story to be told. It is an insight and reality with which we all need to be faced and which hopefully results in raised consciousnesses and healing.

I am so thankful that Dotty and Pat's bringing up allowed their families to embrace their new found family with love and acceptance—as yours have welcomed them.

Please give my love especially to Aunt Margaret—and my appreciation and best wishes to all of you.

Sincerely,

Madelyn Nicholas Sullivan, Florida

Dear Mrs. Haizlip,

It's six a.m. here in Alexandria, as I sit down to write you with the dawn just breaking over the Potomac, voraciously reading your wonderful book *The Sweeter the Juice*, before the work day begins, with all the distractions of family, work.

After forty years of college teaching (including Wellesley College in the early '60s) I am now a retired Professor of Modern Languages Emeritus from Trinity College in D.C. My ancestry is Italian and I was born in Italy and fled the Fascist onslaught in the '30s, settling in New York, getting my graduate degrees from Barnard and Columbia, then marrying a Harvard man (a professor of history) and living the life of academic pilgrims, first in Massachusetts and then in Washington, D.C.

Although I taught all the Romance Languages, my specialty, as was my husband's, was Latin American art and literature.

As a result of hearing you on PBS WETA radio, I went to the library to get your book. It was out, and I put my name on the waiting list, when a good friend from Austin Texas sent it to me as a gift. The day before it arrived in the mail, I had been helping my husband with his research on his Vol. 2 of the *Custis Chronicles*. While looking up wills in Orphans Court Books, at the Alexandria Court House, I accidentally ran across a will written in French from S. Domingo in 1804. It was the will of Bartholomew Dandridge, Jr., and consul to St. Domingo, brother of your Martha (Patty) Washington Dandridge, with an inventory of his possessions and his extensive library.

I am now only on p. 63 of your book and the final coincidence, which made me take pen in hand to write this letter, is that I, Anna Modigliani (married now to James Lynch) still with a Modigliani nose and neck, but no longer with my grey long brown-black hair and always short (never alas tall and elegant in stature) should be reading about Ruth Morris who looked like my distant relative's painting.

I would love to meet you and share with you the ongoing research I am doing for both Alexandria's Black History Resource Center Museum and Alexandria Archeology, along with other dedicated, underpaid and understaffed curators of Alexandria's historic sites, both of African American and other ethnic backgrounds.

My job, as a little grey haired squirrel, is to gather the acorns of primary sources and deposit them in the proper historic "nests" so that others may plant their acorns and grow their family's oak trees.

Congratulating you again on your wonderful story, so engagingly told, I am

　　　　　Sincerely yours,
　　　　　Anna Modigliani Lynch, Virginia

Lost Boundaries

Dear Ms. Haizlip,

I just finished reading your memoir, *The Sweeter the Juice*. A friend of mine (who read an unpublished history I wrote of my father's family that I have entitled *Skeletons in the Closet*) lent your book to me and said she was certain that I would find similarities to my own family. I found it fascinating. First of all, looking through your selection of family pictures, I recognized your uncle, Robert Taylor, as our neighbor in Washington when I was growing up. His daughter "Penny" was around my age, and I remember your uncle coming (in what capacity I do not remember—maybe just to visit) to my father's summer camp in Scotland, Maryland (my father was "the first colored corporal" on the Metropolitan Police Force in Washington and ran Division II of the Police Boys Clubs and Summer Camp II). I remember Mrs. Taylor's "chow-chows."

However, my experience is different in that for years I wanted to track down the descendants of the brother of my maternal grandmother. He had gone to New York City to "pass for white." My father and his sister, my aunt Elinor, always warned me never to try to look them up. If they (i.e. the uncle's descendants) ever found out that they were "colored," they might commit suicide.

After many years of searching, I looked through the indices of the death records of New York City for a Frank or Franklin Kemp, as my father once said he "thought" the son of "Uncle Frank" was also named Frank and was approximately his age. I wrote down the dates of the death of the Frank and Franklin Kemps who were born around the same time as my father, and then looked for obituaries that listed survivors.

I had already found the marriage record of Frank, Sr., and knew that he had married a Maud Cornell. I found a Frank Kemp who died as a young man in 1945 and was survived by a mother Maud and a sister Virginia Hall, in Park Ridge, NJ. I traced Virginia Kemp Hall to Port Charlotte, Florida. At the time I was working on *The Ancestors and Descendants of Martin and Margaret Greenwood, 1470–1985* (they were a German couple who came to America in 1834) and was tracking down all their descendants.

I called Virginia Kemp Hall, who was wildly delighted to make contact with a relative of her father's, as she had never known anything about his family. I learned that neither she nor her late brother had any children. Anyway, she was very friendly over the telephone and even sent me a Christmas card.

Then, the next year I got a call from her. She said that she and her husband were passing through northern Virginia and wanted to meet me. My father and aunt were dead by then and I remembered their warning, "What if they want to meet you? When they find out, they'll kill themselves!" I hemmed and hawed and said that, "You know, my grandmother married a Negro." There was a pause, and she said, "Oh, what the hell!" and they came.

We had a nice talk, in which I never let on that *her father was in fact a Negro*, and showed her pictures only of white-looking relatives. She and her husband departed solemnly and never contacted me again, never answered my letters, never again sent me a Christmas card. Recently I was looking through the computer disks of Social Security cardholders and discovered that she lived another decade after our meeting—until 1996, so I suppose she didn't kill herself.

After I printed the genealogy of the Greenwoods, the genuinely white relatives who had been so helpful on the phone (and in a couple of cases, in person) with about three exceptions, never contacted me again after they learned that one of the sons of Martin and Margaret Greenwood had five children by a free mulatto woman of Norfolk, VA and I was a descendant of that unhallowed union.

So I want to thank you for your book, which, did in fact, enhance memories and also reminded me of similarities in my own family.

Yours sincerely,
Bernard Ruffin, Virginia

Dear Mrs. Haizlip:

Loaned to me by an aunt of mine, I recently read your book, *The Sweeter the Juice*. I caught your initial appearance on the Oprah Winfrey show. It was one interesting hour of television as was your second appearance last summer!

Your family's story is particularly appealing because it is the fabric from which American society is interwoven, the color issue. It has been a subject of controversy for centuries because we essentially know that everyone is indeed not white.

I heard stories about my great-grandfather and his brother, who prior to settling in Gaston County, had been born in Haywood County in the mountains of western North Carolina, near the Cherokee Reservation, where they descended. Leaving the mountains, one went to the black race, and the other headed west to Seattle, Washington, where he entered the white race. I am told that there are members of a white family living there, who share Negro blood with me.

My late grandfather, Hiram Gardin, looked whiter than any white man ever did; yet he did not find it necessary to pass nor did any of his children. I do know that my grandfather's mother was white and that his father, Robert, had at least one Negro ancestor.

My question, then Mrs. Haizlip, is who is really black and who is really white? Your cousins look as white as anyone; yet, they are Negro. I feel that there are many, many white folks passing as something that they are not.

People look at my features, Indian face, tan complexion and fine curly hair and inquire about my ancestry. I cannot simply be Negro; instead, I have to be of some other race, too. It is not possible to be one or the other once I mention the fact that I am black. Mainly, white people have a problem with this. But, blacks do, too.

Mrs. Haizlip, I certainly appreciate your courage to expose your family's deceit and its subsequent effects on your family as a whole, ancestors suddenly disappearing and people, victims of lies, finding out the impossible, that they are and always have been black.

Growing up my father stressed the importance of my watching the famous tearjerker movie, *Imitation of Life*. Coming from a family with one side who looks white and another, who looks Indian, I saw at age twenty-five why. I find it deplorable that the white Hollywood of the '50s chose to cast white Susan Kohner for the role of "Sara Jane" over mulatto, Ellen Holly, who they felt would not draw a sufficient crowd from white moviegoers.

Having seen the film many times, I wonder and vacillate between apathy and empathy for the character. But, I must say this. It is obvious that she did not necessarily desire to be white; instead, she wanted what white represented, equality and opportunity, etc.

Perhaps, this is one justification that passing individuals can use. But, I still feel that if a person has to deny a part of himself, in an attempt to be someone else, he is really not free. Your book helped me better understand this.

I would have given anything to have been in the audience during both of your appearances on *Oprah*. When your white relatives were introduced I could not believe it. Suddenly, America was talking. I would like to believe that we, as a Black people, in terms of color particularly, are beginning to love each other as we are and as we hope to be.

Shirlee, I understand that you are writing part two of your story, which deals with your white relatives and their reaction to your revelation that their great-grandfather, was a slave. Publication date, please!

I am now able to place my adversities with the color issue into perspective because of you and your willingness to share your mother's pain. I thank you and look forward to reading Book II.

May the wind be in your sails, and may God be the wind that blows them. Believe me.

Patrick F. Burris, North Carolina

Dear Mrs. Haizlip,

I had to write after seeing you on *Oprah* and reading *The Sweeter the Juice*—our families are so similar. Like yours, we are racially mixed, predominantly European (Irish) and African. Our two hundred-year saga of life in Virginia and Washington, D.C., *We Were Always Free*, also was published recently. And, we too, had many members who passed for white. However, those of us who chose to stay in the black community never had the desire to seek out those who "crossed over."

Having grown up in Washington D.C.'s apartheid of the 1950s; I share your sentiments about nurturing and acceptance from the black community. I also grew up exposed to excellence in black institutions like Dunbar High and Howard University. Stable, successful black families like TV's Huxtables were not uncommon in our world. So, I've never thought whites were better nor have I longed to claim the white part of my ancestry.

It is ironic that the author of *Who Is Black?* appeared on Oprah's show with you. I briefly corresponded with him about our different views on the one-drop rule. Though identity with the black race is indelibly printed on my psyche, my young relatives growing up in a less insular world may not feel so exclusively bonded. I also concede that the one-drop rule is unscientific and illogical; Latino and Asian immigrants who've questioned my black label have brought about that realization.

Nevertheless, I defend the one-drop rule as serving a vital role in our evolution towards racial equality. We may be the only people in the world who adhere to the one drop rule, but we are also the only mixed race people that affirms its black bloodline.

When one looks at other hybrids with a black component—in North Africa, the Americas or elsewhere—the more negroid or black looking people are at the bottom of a hierarchy, with whites or near whites on top. It is instructive to examine the racial history of Mexicanos/Chicanos, one hybrid group in close proximity to us. As pointed out in your book, Los Angeles was founded by a largely black and mulatto group from Mexico. However, their descendants are not classified as black as we are.

Though 200,000 Africans brought to colonial Mexico were absorbed into the Indian and Spanish communities there, those Africans have been exorcised from the history, memory, and psyche of Mexican people. Mexicans were once classified in census records according to all their racial lineage—which is the aim of some bi- and multi-racial Americans with black ancestry. Yet, later on Mexicans could and would change their race to deny the black bloodline, if their phenotype so allowed.

One Chicano Studies professor told me that Mexicanos/ Chicanos do not speak of Mexico's black heritage because it had been bred out. But, has it? Maybe the black element survives as a shadow that emerges in anti-black sentiment Mexican writers admit exists in their society. Is this what's to become of Americans with black ancestry?

The growing movement to acknowledge all of our racial parts leaves many African Americans fearful that one day there won't be any black people in America—a kind of genocide. Are those calling themselves bi- and multi-racial (I'll refer to them as BMR) merely seeking to claim all of their racial parts or are they also seeking to distance themselves from the black community?

If their aim is the former then the BMRs should stop promoting the mythology that they are different from the majority of African Americans. After all, at least 75% of us are also bi- or multi-racial. And, racially mixed people are nothing new. Moreover, the BMRs should understand that despite a different label, the greater society will perceive most of them as African Americans and treat them accordingly.

In *Who Is Black?* Dr. Davis offers Hawaii as a model for redefining America's racially mixed people. But, Hawaii's dirty little secret is that its darkest people endure routine racial discrimination. While we make room for other definitions of race, the one-drop rule can be viewed as a therapeutic stopgap that serves to honor the part of humanity universally denied and denigrated.

To have America confront the fact of black genes in the white population, as you have done, is also therapeutic. Why should a person, on learning he has black ancestry, feel distressed about it? And, why should the person in question face betrayal from associates who learn of his black heritage? Thank you for your contribution to racial healing in writing *The Sweeter the Juice.*

> Sincerely,
> Sandra D. Madden, California

Hello Mrs. Haizlip:

I just completed reading your wonderful book, *The Sweeter the Juice*. I am also writing because I married into a family who have members who have gone over to the white world. I have enclosed some pictures of this family which was started over 150 years ago in this town by a white man named Matthew Fields and a 3/4 Indian and 1/4 black woman named Rilley Wade.

She had nine children for Mr. Fields and to his credit he told the town whites that all of his children were colored. When he died he left his considerable fortune to his nine children. He is buried in a black cemetery. To our knowledge only Sylvia of his generation went over to the white world because she left this town as a young woman and never returned.

The story of how your mother's family went over to the other side reminded me of an incident that took place in South Carolina about 40 years ago. There was this fair skinned family that had two daughters. One daughter was married to a dark skinned man while the other daughter was single. The single daughter left and moved to New York but continued to write to her family.

One day they received a letter stating that she was coming home to get her sister and husband and move to New York where Negro people were treated much better than in the south. The sister came and they packed the Model T with their belongings and started on their way. About 5 miles outside of town the married sister's hat "blew" off her head and her husband got out of the car to retrieve it. When he bent down to pickup the hat they drove away and left him standing there.

They wrote to their parents for a while but never gave a return address and eventually the letters stopped and they were never heard from again. Everyone figured they went over in the white world.

This is a great country but I'll always believe that racism will keep her from being all she can be. (Unless of course we make race a non-issue in our society.)

Robert Washington, North Carolina

Dear Mrs. Haizlip,

I have just completed the book, *The Sweeter the Juice*. What a great experience to share with other people.

As I read the book, I found a very amazing comparative with our families' evolutions.

My parents hale from small coal mining towns in West Virginia. My father is of a latter end of nine siblings, four of which that have gone on to paradise. My father Curtis, who is affectionately known as Curt to family, friends as well as new acquaintances. The Shepherd clan or "my nation" as my father puts it abounds with clergy, educators and labors. All very proud and knowledgeable of the family lineage and it begins in Virginia as a freed slave who took the name Shepherd from his former owner.

The family somehow migrated to West Virginia where an intermingle of Indian blood is present in my fraternal grandmother's side. The stories along with aged pictures of this beautiful proud black/Indian family have been indoctrinated into the memories of all the grandchildren as well as my teenage son.

My mother's family history is somewhat obscure. My ninety-two-year-old grandmother speaks ill of her late husband, whom she married at the age of twenty-three. My grandfather was a widower with five children. Seven years later my mother was born along with two brothers. Although my mother is close to her family and some of her half siblings, there is definitely some disparity amongst the children. And with that, it leaves unanswered questions of my complete heritage.

My mother's family is very fair. People have on occasion questioned my racial background. After reading your book I have come to realize and acknowledge that I am just as caucasian as Martha Washington, as Indian as Pocohantas, and as black as Shaka Zulu. Does it matter to me the portions of my heritage, no because I am made of the best of everything. The God of my salvation created and fashioned me with his great and wondrous powers. That is all I and others need to know.

Thank you for sharing such an enlightening and personal part of your life.

Sincerely,
Deidre B. Shepherd, Michigan

Dear Mrs. Haizlip:

Let me start by saying how much I enjoyed your book *The Sweeter the Juice.* I found it interesting, entertaining and moving. It touched my heart, and the information that you were able to find out about your mother's family and the reuniting of the sisters made me face some demons of my own in my family.

I can identify with the feeling of loss and sadness that your mother must have felt all of those years feeling rejected by her family. I too have that feeling of loss. I am an Afro-American woman, but for the past twenty-five years I have wondered where and what has happened to my father's family. My father abandoned my mother and myself when I was a year old and I have not had any contact with him or any of my relatives from his side of the family.

My question to you is how can I go about locating a missing family? What would be my first steps in discovering my roots? I have never even seen pictures of my grandparents or brother from my father's previous marriage. I would like to know what can I do, if anything to find my family, maybe find out where I can get pictures of great-great relatives, and get some closure to this situation which has been very painful to me all of my life. Thank you for your time and may God continue to bless you in your life and all that you do.

> Sincerely,
> Lisa Tolliver-Burke, New Orleans
> and New York

Dear Mrs. Haizlip,

To be honest, I must say that to be fair to those who "pass for white" (a phrase I argue in my book *Jane's Way* should be relegated to those who cosmetically alter their appearance, not those whose genetic makeup is predominantly white) one must take into account the obstacle or burden that their black ancestry has been for them which depends on the time and place one is born into, which is different for everyone.

Quite frankly, I don't think a graduate of Wellesley who grew up in Connecticut, has held several executive positions, and lives in an expensive home in sunny California has been greatly hindered by that heritage, and therefore perhaps not in the best possible position to ask the question "why would someone want to 'pass for white'?"

My character, Jane Weston, did not grow up with many positive role models of color in Red Hook, Brooklyn, unlike yourself, the daughter of well-educated and respected parents, a minister and his wife. Any newspaper or television article will show you negative images and stereotypes, and unfortunately, there are those who perpetuate them by acting them out. Jane is a woman of great pride and ambition, and wants no part of the "homeboys," nor does she want any such stereotype applied to her. She does not claim to be white, she simply lets people assume she is, but does admit to being mixed if pressed.

Anyone who has seen *Pinky* and other such films knows how poorly one could be treated if that ancestry is revealed, even if the person in question hasn't gone to great lengths to conceal it. Your older relatives lived in more hostile times and perhaps territories and one can understand why they might not like to be treated the way Pinky was every day of their lives.

Moreover, as you point out, most if not all "white" Americans have some African ancestry and could be accused of "passing" without realizing it. The only difference I can see is that your relatives knew about it. By the same token, one could accuse you of "passing" without realizing it because unless you said it or wrote it on a form, no one would know about it and judge you that way. Even Queen Elizabeth II has some long-ago African ancestry, but as you point out, it would be ludicrous to point it out to someone who has absolutely no concept of what it means to be black.

As far as any great inner torment suffered by those who "pass," Jane would find that as ludicrous an inquiry as asking why she would want to. . . . Jane would simply say that there wasn't one damned thing on the other side of the color line that she wanted. She had a mother from whom she felt alienated and a grandmother whose coddling she outgrew. On the other side, she has a millionaire father and an English Duke for a husband. Let any resident of Harlem, Watts or Red Hook top that. Readers can call it snobbery if they want, but honestly, would you rather be a have or have not?

(I'm still working on the last chapter of the book, but will send you a copy once it's copyrighted, if you wish.)

Sincerely,
Tom LaSalle, New York

Dear Mrs. Haizlip:

I recently purchased your book *The Sweeter the Juice* and have thoroughly enjoyed reading it. My enjoyment comes from the belief that somehow we are related. Unfortunately I have not been able to trace my family history like you did.

My family are descendants of the Morrises and Scotts. The Morrises are originally from Lowmoor, Virginia, but moved to Coleman Falls, Virginia, about 20 miles outside Lynchburg, Virginia. From what my grandmother remembers, her grandmother was a slave to a white immigrant, named John Morris, believed to be from Ireland. During this time, Clara Morris, my grandmother's mother, and Mr. Morris had several children.

My grandmother's parents names were LuLu and Tyler

Morris. Because my grandmother is 96 years old, she does not remember any of the other relatives. It is believed that after slavery ended, John Morris returned to Ireland.

I was recently in Pittsburgh, Pennsylvania, visiting my aunt and uncle, who have also purchased your book, and we were discussing the similarities of the families. My uncle mentioned that he remembered mention of a great-uncle who had lived in the Baltimore-Washington area in the 1800s. My uncle said that there was never any communication with this relative because it was believed that he was "passing for white" and would not risk entertaining his darker relatives.

There was some family property that other relatives wanted to sell and we attempted to find him or his descendants, but to no avail.

Your description of "your" Morris family is exactly that of "my" Morris family. I remember when my grandfather died, there was a knock at the door and my mother asked me to see who it was. The gentleman identified himself as "William Morris." My mother asked me who it was and I said I didn't know, but it was some white man by the name of William Morris. Since I had never met the man before, I was unaware that he was my cousin and a black man.

My mother later asked me why did I say that he was a white man and I said that he had sandy, curly hair and grey eyes and the only other people that I had seen that looked like him were white.

In your book, you have some pictures that could have come from our family album. The picture of Grace Morris Cramer shows a distinct family resemblance to my great-aunt Aurelia Davis; the picture of Margaret Maher Morris favors my grandmother, Lottie Scott; the picture of Roberta Fortune Taylor resembles my cousin, Brenda Scott Ingram. I am sure that you have noticed mention of the Scott name. My grandmother married William Scott. Unfortunately, to our knowledge, most of the Scott family is deceased.

To add another twist to this, my cousin, Doris Morris, married a man named Calvin Taylor, who is from North Carolina. I am going to talk to my cousin Calvin about this family.

If at all possible, I would particularly like for you to talk with my uncle in Pittsburgh or my mother in Lynchburg. Since you have completed your research you may know how or what questions to ask my uncle or mother that would help us further trace our family tree.

Take care and I hope to be talking with you soon.

Thomasine Linda Butler, Maryland

Dear Mrs. Haizlip:

I read the fine review of your book in the *Los Angeles Times* and found it in my local bookstore.

Just completed the chapter on your father, Rev. Julian Taylor, which I read with tears in my eyes. Your pride in him and in your family rings through the book. It reads like a novel and I am truly moved by it.

As a fellow long-term "American" I believe firmly your theory that if we would all accept how racially mixed we all are — maybe we could all recognize each other as struggling human beings. Langston Hughes was right! Varying shades of beige will be better!

A similar "secret" seems to exist in my family. My mother was a very fair skinned redhead who married a very dark-skinned, wavy-haired man. All of us looked like our Mom but I always wondered at my father's difference from his own family of fair skin and dark-haired individuals. Both sides of the family came from the South (Oklahoma, Kentucky, and Tennessee).

My paternal aunt discounts any "mixed" blood as she does her genealogies of the paternal "English" side. However, my father always said there was Cherokee blood, which my great-uncle told him about. My friend (half-Cherokee) said when she saw family pictures, "Your father looks like a full-blood Cherokee, where was his family from?" HMMMMM! Your excellent book has whetted my curiosity about denial in my own family and my own father's sense of "less than" in a color based family and society.

Just wanted to share that with you *and* let you know how I am enjoying your story. Somewhere I know, Margaret feels better about herself and what happened to her. May many read it—it's a necessary and thought-provoking book. My congratulations!

Patricia E. Watson, California

Dear Ms. Haizlip:

I've never felt motivated to respond directly to an author's work. This time, however, I must write. I just finished reading *The Sweeter the Juice* five minutes ago. I'm sure you've had many strangers tell you how important this book has been for them, but somehow I think you won't mind another thank-you.

For the past week I've been engrossed in your bold and thoughtful trek through our collective American racial morass. The search for "mystic chords of memory" continues to shape my American experience as I continue to search for distant and not-so-distant biological relatives, white and black. As a light-skinned twenty-five year old biracial woman who was adopted by a white family, I know something of the frenetic dance of trying to pin yourself down in history.

Thank you for giving me a family memoir that gives historical and personal context to the lives of the racially dis-membered. Your book digs beneath tired-out literary tragic mulatto stereotypes to reveal *individuals* who make day-to-day decisions based on the world spinning around them.

When I found my white biological mother almost six years ago, I had expected to find an "average white girl." Well, this "average white girl" turned out to be part of one of the oldest, wealthiest "Mayflower" families in the country.

I continue to search for my biological father, a handsome, dignified-looking man from St. Louis. Both of them, in surprising and annoying persistence, revisit me every day as I look into the mirror. To me, that's America. Please know how very important this book is to me. You have made a first step in a meadow where God is waiting.

My Very Best Wishes,
Hawley Fogg-Davis, New York

Dear Mrs. Haizlip:

I recently read *The Sweeter the Juice* and have been so moved by your story that I feel compelled to write to you.

Your family memoirs brought to the surface long buried memories of incidents in my life as a negro who could have chosen to "go over." I recall seeing, only once, an uncle who went over; I also recall racial jokes and slurs made in my presence by ones who thought I was white; I remember stories told to me when I was very young, of the lynchings and other atrocities committed by the Ku Klux Klan; I remember my father deciding not to go to his birthplace in Alabama for the burial of his father because of the harsh treatment of negroes there; I recall that while on a date, my sister, her brown skinned escort and I were denied admission to a movie house, because as the ticket seller said, "We don't allow colored people in this movie." This was in Pittsburgh, Pennsylvania.

As I grew to adulthood, I was made aware of the prejudice in job hiring. One of the largest department stores (Kaufmann's) in

Pittsburgh hired me as the first black sales lady, unaware that a black lady had been working in their jewelry department for years. During the Depression my best friend got a job in a drugstore as a clerk by passing. An envious acquaintance of hers told the owner that she was black and she was fired.

People of color who have lived in America all have a story to tell. I am in your mother's generation and felt deeply her sadness in not being able to grow up with her sister. The family reunion was a happy ending. I hope they have a good relationship now.

Sincerely,
Selma Gilmore, California

Dear Simon and Schuster:

The wonderfully written book by Shirlee Taylor Haizlip, *The Sweeter the Juice*, has helped me cope with my blackness. I am very light and for many years even as a young child I was never accepted by white or black people. Your book allowed me to look inside myself and realize I am not alone.

Thank you Mrs. Haizlip for letting me into your family history and making me feel a deeper relationship with my color. I'm black and never denied it but friends, family, lovers always made me feel guilty. Employers look at me and think I'm white but what they don't know is that I'm black. You talk about your white side and it was nice to hear that from you. I've been fighting with myself over my black and white side for so long. This problem has caused me to be hospitalized and it's mentally drained me.

Words cannot express how much I thank you. I'm twenty-three years old and I feel confident about myself more so than I ever did before. I'm going back to school and I feel spiritually strong and mentally capable. Thank you for your book.

Thank you so much!!!
John Reece McClanahan, Illinois

Dear Ms. Haizlip,

Our class read and discussed the introduction of your book *The Sweeter the Juice*. The students had a lively discussion about the issues of race and family described in your story. The ending of your introduction was especially meaningful for them.

As part of our classroom activities, students were asked to create a "This is a story" poem to share their own family experiences. Enclosed you will find two packets of their efforts. The first one in each group is a community poem. Students selected a line from their work to create one that represented the ideas, values, attitudes, and beliefs of the entire class. Each class has signed its joint effort for you.

A word about our school: The Wilbur Cross High Annex is an educational program that started eight weeks ago. Its mission is to provide at-risk students with an accelerated, interdisciplinary, team-taught educational experience that helps them gain the credits they need to graduate from high school. Finding reading material and assignments that are stimulating is very challenging. The provocative dialogue generated by your writing is one of our earliest teaching successes.

Sincerely yours,
Michael M. Brownstein and Gail Staggers,
New Haven, Connecticut

Connections Not Surprising

Dear Mrs. Haizlip:

Thank you for *The Sweeter the Juice*. I have just read it. It is wonderful.

It took me a bit of effort to find the book. I heard part of the

Public Radio piece (getting in the car after it began and having to leave the car before it was over). I tracked you down through our local Public Radio station I heard enough to get the general outline of what your book was about, and not a lot more. I did not even know your name. I am telling you all of this because my Public Radio station was very helpful. I told the customer service person the little I knew (expecting to be sent on to the East Coast affiliate). The customer service person was great. She finished my sentence for me, instantly. She gave me the information I needed to order the book. She said, "There have been so many calls about this book, I am keeping the information right here on my desk." I thought you might like to know that.

I was particularly interested in your book because of my own life. I grew up in New York. I was born in 1934 on Long Island. My maiden name was Mortensen. When you grow up in New York and your name is Mortensen, you are asked several times a month if you are Jewish. It was seldom an ugly question. It was just informational. The answer to this question (answers from my father's sister or from my mother responding to the questioners) was "Oh, no. It is an old Danish name. Jews spell it . . . on. Danes spell it . . . en. We are Danish."

In 1983 my mother told me (prior to her imminent open heart surgery) that she discovered a letter indicating my father's family was Jewish (Danish Jews). She said she'd discovered the letter the night before.

It took a few years, a lot of searching, and a considerable amount of pain before I found that she had found such a letter, but it was a great many years before. After that, an elderly cousin of my father's gave me a copy of my Mortensen family's genealogy, documenting our Jewish heritage back to 1640.

I have been in a relatively continual and mostly fruitless religious search for most of my life, even as a child. I have finally found my morality is Jewish (and always has been). My father gave me his morality; he just left all the labels off that morality. No wonder I found it difficult to locate a match with what I believed, really believed. My mother (who is eighty-one) has never once in my hearing uttered the word "God." She was a failed or lapsed Catholic. I have no idea if she even believes in a Supreme Being.

I will become a Jew in a formal ceremony quite soon.

I have been dealing with the amputation of my heritage and recovery of my heritage since 1983. It has been a very painful process. My mother no longer speaks to me. This process of alienation began when it became apparent that I would explore that Jewish heritage to find what belonged to me. My brother has demanded that I not speak to his grown children about my discovery of our Jewish heritage, information (it seems) he has had for many, many years.

Last year I decided I had whined to the people I was allowed to speak to about this (few in my immediate family but probably everyone else in my world, even the United Parcel man) for far too long. I was going to whine no longer. People who write journals have better mental health than most of us. I needed a little improvement of my mental health. I decided I would write a journal; I'd put down all those feelings. And so I wrote, and wrote, and wrote, and wrote.

And it was a great help. My laptop sang. My pain was lessened. . . .

Thank you for your scholarship and for your industry. Thank you for your openness and your wonderful candor. Thank you for your courage. My brother does not want to be Jewish. He will surely not speak to me, again, if this is published. Thank you for helping me see being open and honest about one's heritage is the most appropriate posture in the long

run. Thank you for helping me through the confusing feelings and to have the courage to go on a bit further in this effort. . . .
> Sincerely yours,
> B. T., New Mexico

(Author's note: The locations, name, and initials in this letter have been changed.)

Dear Mrs. Haizlip:

My daughter loaned me your book, *The Sweeter the Juice,* which I enjoyed very much. However, just enjoying a book is not sufficient reason to write the author. I felt that you had elucidated the situation of people who care about their heritage, and live in "two worlds" at the same time. While I am Jewish, and white, I feel the tension between economic (and social) advantage in the majority culture, and living as part of my own people. My family could easily have "passed" into the majority culture because we have long since shed the accents and mannerisms of the Eastern European shtetl. (Of course, dark toned African Americans don't usually have that option.) In addition, we are of the same generation: I was born in 1932.

Through some personal friends, I find that there are similar dynamics within the Native American communities. My wife and I attended a panel discussion at Haverford College featuring several Native American composers who work in the "white" world, but want to put some of their heritage into their music.

To complicate the simple solutions of the past, we have also come in contact with several African-American Jews. These people have another dimension of ethnicity; although they seem to be evolving towards main stream Jewish identity and practice. In some recent discussions with an Armenian-American lady, I gather that her very traditional Armenian Church has several members who are not Armenian at all, as well as those who married into the Armenian community. This is good; people should be welcomed into Armenian, Jewish, or African American circles (as did your grandmother), with mutual acceptance by the group they wish to enter. Ethnicity should be an enlargement of an individual being, not a trap into which a person is forced by the larger, non-ethnic, society.

My son-in-law is from Montreal, and has roots in both the Polish and Italian Jewish cultures. As a music teacher, he is preparing for Martin Luther King Day at a largely Afro-American school. To help him out, since he is not aware of the Freedom Struggle in the '60s, my wife has been going through some tapes of songs from that period. The beautiful thing about that period was that many people were fighting for the freedom of others, not just for themselves. To quote Rabbi Hillel from the Talmud, "If I am not for myself, who will be for me. But if I am for myself alone, what am I?"

My wife, Elaine, and I have been working on sustainability for about twenty-five years now. Sustainability means keeping us all from destroying the things on Planet Earth that make a good life possible for so many people. We have organized five annual conferences at colleges in the Philadelphia area on this problem. One of the understandings that has emerged is that a sustainable world is probably a multi-ethnic world. Perhaps, you can help spread these ideas around the circles in which you move.

That would be working for all of us, as individuals, as members of our respective ethnic groups, and as grandparents who want a good life for future generations.

> Shalom (peace),
> Ernest B. Cohen, P.E. and Ph.D.,
> Pennsylvania

Dear Ms. Haizlip,

You probably will not receive this letter but I'm compelled to write anyway. I just read *The Sweeter the Juice* and found it not only interesting and well written, but important. I enjoyed it on its own merits, but for personal reasons as well. There are similarities between what your family members did in passing for white, and what my parents did in trying to pass for non-Jews. Of course, it's infinitely more difficult to be black than Jewish in this society, but the fear of exposure and having to be on guard were true for my family as well.

My parents didn't want Jewish problems, had negative feelings about Jews, and wanted to convert to Christianity, so they broke with family when I was about 10. Their parents were dead but close sibling relationships ended abruptly, and they told my sister and me not to tell people we were Jewish. I obeyed easily, until grown, when many things began to bother me. I've had to overcome my fears and learned prejudices against Jews. At 58 I'm in limbo—not feeling like a Jew because I have no right to claim it, yet thinking, knowing, and saying (mostly to people who are tired of hearing it) that I am Jewish.

You wrote, "But at what cost. . . . What did such distancing and denial of one's self as well as of an entire group of people do to the mind and the soul?" My answer is that the cost was very high, and it certainly damaged *my* mind and soul. My parents are gone so I can never learn what I need to know of my ancestors and I have not yet succeeded in finding even one person from my father's large "poor, uneducated, low-class" and apparently unacceptable side of the family, even though there has been some connection with my mother's family.

My own family is beautifully diverse; our daughter's husband is black Panamanian and our son's wife is Filipino. We have the most adorable biracial grandchildren and we're thrilled with all our kids. I do understand why blacks or Jews, or anyone else in this society would want to "pass." People are bigots and life is hard enough without costly discrimination. But how can one deny who they are, and how can they deny heritage to their children?

At an early age I felt strongly about prejudice and about all inequality, but not until recently did efforts to become involved succeed. Long before my interest due to our multi-racial family, my concern was there. Recently friends and I formed a human relations group and it's extremely fulfilling.

My mother and I met with relatives after a 30-year separation. Mother wanted not to be found, hated the new contacts, and later said she wished she had never acknowledged who she was when they located her, mainly because I reacted favorably and found more of her family. (They must have felt anger towards us, but how kind they were about it. My aunt asked, "Why did your family have to completely break with us? Why couldn't they simply convert?" I told her "we apparently couldn't be 'non Jews,' and have Jewish relatives.")

Best wishes always to you and your wonderful family. I will be looking for a sequel.

Susan Robertson, California

Dear Shirlee,

I just finished reading your book and it was a tour de force. In no particular order, I was impressed with the skill of your writing, your formidable memory (although you did leave out any description of Biology 101 and your erstwhile lab partner) and your remarkable insights as to the complexity of black-white relationships that go far beyond gene pools.

Your book raised such basic issues about identity that it should be read for that alone. After we move from our own personality and reality which we take from our genetic makeup, our family, our marriage, work, etc. and move into the community to which we think we belong, how much is intrinsic, and how much is imposed from the external world?

It is hard for me to rely on genetic contributions from my ancestors as supporting my identity; perhaps because I can trace my background back only two generations on one level and almost 6000 years on another. Because Jews were expelled from so many countries and continents in their history and yet lived all over the world and intermarried with every population they were in contact, physical appearance is meaningless to identity. One has only to go to Israel to see this. In five minutes, on any busy street, the U.N. passes before one's eyes; yet they are all Jews.

Certainly there is nothing about the appearance of an Ethiopian or Russian or Indian or Australian Jew that suggests a common history or gene pool with any other Jew. And yet we are all linked through history and common belief. Should that not be the linkage between all of us, regardless of our skin color?

I was also thinking of those in your family who have passed and how difficult it must be to know how to relate to them. At what point do they stop being a member of your extended family? This has personal relevance to me as my oldest niece has just converted to Greek Orthodoxy in preparation for her marriage to a first generation Greek she met at college. Her children and her grandchildren certainly will never think of themselves as Jewish. And my father, my niece's grandfather, will become as remote to her children as the black members of your family were to the grandchildren of Grace. There will be no common ground on which the different arms of the family will meet except a sharing of a history too remote to be meaningful.

My best,

Judith J. Wurtman, Ph.D., Massachusetts

(Author's note; Judith was my ever-inquisitive laboratory partner at Wellesley College in Biology 101.)

Dear Shirlee (first-name basis but I have an intuitive soul and I know from your warm commentary that we are family! Don't worry, I won't be descending on you.) (chuckle)

I am a very blessed man of sixty years. Blessed because I have lived among Brothers and Sisters and socialized when there was opportunity. My soul is Black and Jewish. White folks have *no* idea of the warmth and beauty of most brothers and sisters. And the humor AMEN!

After all we oppressed people have to have some compensation from God for the way the dominant society has treated us.

Today, I thought, thank God Colin Powell didn't run for president. Such a gentleman deserves better. Why should he fight against a river of scum? Americans will find another president. I have a thirty-year-old daughter who helps Russian Jews in San Francisco. She also loves black culture. Probably gets it from her old man. Also a son twenty-eight who is in charge of computers for a firm in Connecticut. My wife is an RN. Yes, I would love to see how all my ancestors looked.

Warm regards,
Alvin F. Rubin, Rhode Island

P.S. The Mishnah says that Jews were originally people of color. Thank God! (Chuckle)

Dear Shirlee:

You must have received numbers of letters from former Wellesley classmates, following publication of your book: here is another.

I write to thank you for telling your story as you have. In addition to its power as a narrative of black/white relations, it has resonances well beyond these, into what is no longer just an American but is increasingly a global issue of social and individual identity. I identified with it in part because of my own immediate ancestry, with one grandfather who abandoned the family when my father was seven, and the other who disguised his Russian (undoubtedly Jewish) immigrant past, marrying an orphan, who died when my mother was two—thereby being able to carry off his disguise until long after his death, when a distant maternal cousin, in pursuit of family genealogy, uncovered his "forswearing of allegiance to the Czar" on his marriage certificate.

Anyway, there was a lot of general disappearance and denial—and *mutatis mutandis,* for my parents respectively, a lot of self-making which became so much of my family "heritage" that it would be almost impossible for me to trace a family tree as extensively as you have yours. Thus I have some understanding even if it is in a different sphere. I have more understanding of it after finishing your book—and I hope, as I continue in my academic career as a sociologist at the City University of New York, to exemplify the greater wisdom you have facilitated.

I write not only to thank you but also to ask more about your experience at Highland Beach. . . . In the process of my research, I have talked with my Montclair friend who is at least 4th generation in a home in Highland Beach. She explained to me why her mother and sister inherited it when their two brothers had no such share: the brothers passed, in the 1930's, and while no one blamed them for doing so in order to get work, it was understood that they would never come back to the beach. Your own family history, again.

Understood more broadly, however, that phenomenon has resonated in other case studies of respondents I have interviewed in New England: if you don't want to "get in touch with who you are" (as one respondent put it to me) as a WASP, you choose not to come back to the place and may even hope/expect to be bought out by those who do so identify with their "tribe" (if only for a week or two every summer). You may deliberately marry someone who will take you out. . . .

I am trying to tease out an understanding of individual decisions made regarding familial issues, which are themselves imbedded in community/ethnic/racial parameters. Invariably, the people who respond to my inquiries are the survivors—those who have stayed the course and continued to identify with the family (if not necessarily more broadly with the "tribe") . . .

At very least, accept my gratitude for your book and what it has done to advance my understanding—and that of others—of the complexities of the human condition in general and the racial situation in America in particular.

Sincerely,
Judy Huggins Balfe, Ph.D., New York City

(Author's note: I remember fondly Judy's ever thoughtful questions in classes we shared.)

Dear Shirlee,

Whenever I have a chance, I look through your book. I always thoroughly examine the photographs, which intrigue me so.

Your story had me on the edge of my chair throughout the duration. As a Jewish woman, I also know what it means to have relations who "hide" who they are. Even though my skin is white, inside I often feel very different from other Americans around me.

When my great great grandparents fled the persecutions of Russia, the first thing they changed was their name. I am told that their experiences in the "old" country were so terrifying that many in our family refused to speak of our heritage once the boat arrived safely in New York Harbor. So many missing links.

I have begun collecting old family photos. I search and study their faces for a clue of who they were and what they hoped for and loved. How much I admire your persistence and dedication. You are an inspiring woman, Shirlee—and I feel fortunate to have heard your story firsthand. . . . I would love for my children to meet you one day.

> Best Wishes,
> Rebecca A. Sher, Massachusetts

Dear Ms. Haizlip,

I'm so glad that you have selected the all too conservative Orange County as one of your stops. I was deeply moved listening to your story and motivation for this book.

I know about "passing." As a young girl growing up in Orange County, I found out quickly that it wasn't acceptable to be different. I was a little Jewish girl with jet-black curly hair, brown eyes and olive skin. Hate came my way . . . Dirty Jew, Christ Killer, Ugly. The pain and the shame were enormous; it seemed easier to pass.

Only recently have I fully understood the tremendous ramification of denying that which I am.

Over the past few years, I began reading books by African American women authors. I love the power, strength, wisdom and tenacity these women have expressed and shared through their writing.

I didn't have a strong, supportive family growing up. I am learning the lessons of being a proud, strong, loving, and forgiving woman through the sharing of women's wisdom.

We can only hope to defuse racism, sexism through enlightenment. Thank you for sharing and adding to my life. God bless you and your family.
Love,
Jeannie Breslin, California

I, like so many other readers, read Shirley Taylor Haizlip's book because of the implications it had for my family. I am the aunt of two gorgeous little children who are true "Heinz 57" variety of white, Hispanic, black, Native American, gentile, and Jew. To the members of our family, they are simply two more children to love and cherish. Unfortunately, to the members of our society, they are two children who are viewed with suspicion because they do not easily fit into any one racial category.

I wince every time I hear well meaning people make comments like, "Your nephew is such a beautiful child! He could easily pass for white. Pity his sister won't, not with that hair." Equally disturbing are observations from my niece that go along these lines, "Daddy and I are brown, but everyone else in the family is white; why?" Neither child should grow up feeling the need to "pass" itself off as anything: rich, poor, white or black.

In a family that has never made distinctions between its members based on skin color, it saddens me that one of its youngest members has learned to do so in pre-school. I pray that our society will learn to see and judge its members based on who they are and how they behave, not based on what race they do or do not belong [to]. It should not be a liability to be something other than "white."

Perhaps, as more of us discover our richly mixed heritage, as Haizlip has done, we will be able to throw away our race and color labels. Considering the pride and acceptance these people have shown in their family heritage, I believe my prayers may actually be answered. Who knows, it may one day be common-place to see a brown child hugging a tow-headed child and proudly announcing," This is my cousin, and we love each other."

Sincerely,

Jennifer J. A. Pavio, New York

Dear Mrs. Taylor Haizlip

I am a stranger to you, yet I've become an admirer though your book *The Sweeter the Juice.* I found yours to be a profoundly moving story, being compelled by its content, and enjoying your musical use of language.

You caused me to travel with you through your family history and personal experiences. In fact, I was very sorry to come to the end of the book, as I savored each page, particularly toward the conclusion. You see, I often saw bits and pieces of my own life, however dimly reflected, in your travels.

I am a Caucasian American New Yorker, of Alsatian, Danish, and German descent. I've had a loving relationship for nearly twenty years, sixteen of which married, with a beautiful South Carolinian black woman. We have two wonderful daughters, ages ten and eight. Being in the arts, my wife is an opera singer; we have lived in Berlin, Germany for eight years. Coincidentally enough, she did her grade schooling in Hartsville, South Carolina, and we lived our first years together on West 80th Street in Manhattan.

I could never presume to know truly what it is like to walk in the shoes of a person of color. I must admit I was a slow learner at first, but particularly after the births and now raising of our daughters, my steps often come close enough to have some idea.

Living among the Germans too is a bit of stranger in a strange land feeling.

With so many media exploited events such as the Simpson verdict and "Million Man March" in the news, I often think of my not so distant ignorant past, and see from where I've come as being a new life. When you spoke of your inherited mantle of integration slipping low these days and often tripping you up, I wanted to say something to you of hope and being strong. However, I often despair of the possibilities for change when I feel and see the tide against it. I can only steel myself against the ignorant and keep my own faith.

I am deeply protective of my children's experiences, but realize they must go through it themselves at some point, hopefully with their self-esteem and spirits intact. How to create a balanced openness through it all is the challenge.

You have written an important book that is also timely. A real American story of the best and the worst in us, and American society. Thank you for sharing your story, and enriching my life. It is a journey all should take with you. Let us hope.

Steven Willemann, Berlin, Germany

Dear Shirlee,

I hope you don't mind using your first name, but after reading your book *The Sweeter the Juice* it seems like I've known you on that level. I found it in the new book section of our mostly lily-white community library. Mostly white Christian Anglo-Saxon liberals who gravitated to one of the nicest places in the country to live populate the town of Ketchum. However, there are very few other ethnic groups in the area.

I'm a third generation Japanese-American and grew up in San Jose, California, after spending my first three years behind barbed wire in Topaz, one of ten concentration camps which was located 110 miles south of Salt Lake City, Utah. Unlike you, I can trace my ethnically unbroken family history back for centuries to feudal Japan. Unbroken, that is, until the birth of my son, Chris, whose mother was of French and German descent. Perhaps he could also have some black blood in his system?

As a member of a relatively smaller minority group, I experienced some of the negatives that come with race that you mentioned in the book. The main one being the inferiority of not quite measuring up to the white standards of physical beauty. I knew I wasn't a John Wayne and identified with the Indians. In fact, today I attend and dance at powwows and am accepted by the Native-Americans as a brother. I've met "mixed breeds" of European, African, Native-American and Hispanic background, but no other Asians other than one man whose father was Japanese-American. The small children often have an Asian look.

My first experience with overt racism was when my family returned to live in the Fillmore section of San Francisco, which is where the Japanese area had existed since the early 1900's. During World War II, many southern blacks moved into it when shipyard jobs were plentiful. I was called names, punched and spit on by black kids for looking like the former enemy. Finally, a big kid put me on his shoulders and warned the others that I was under his protection. After my older brother, Sheldon, died in a tonsil operation, my folks decided to move to a then agricultural San Jose and I received my first taste of "equal opportunity" discrimination from white kids.

I realize that things haven't changed in many areas of race relations, but you have to admit that it's getting better in others. Less than thirty years ago, I could not have been married and divorced from a white woman in this state. I received majority custody of our son and have been raising him as a single parent. And I can't "pass."

I am happy that you were able to find Grace Cramer and

the Scotts. Kenneth and his kids accept you as family. Isn't that what it's all about? I have three sisters and a brother. One sister, Arlene, is married to Gene, a white razorback from Arkansas, who claims a little Cherokee. Valerie is married to Carl Sermon, whose father came from Austria as a child. Sheridan married Muneko, from Japan (their daughter, Shoko, is the only "ethnically pure" child in the family). The youngest, Melanie, married Ron, of Irish stock. Interactions between the different family groups are good.

I thoroughly enjoyed reading your family memoir. It was instructive and captivating. I, too, will be looking for something other than "Indian" when I gaze at white people.

> Sincerely,
> Rod Tatsuno, Idaho

Dear Rebecca Saletan, (Simon & Schuster)

Having read *The Sweeter the Juice,* I was excited to learn it was one of your books. You see my grandmother and her sister had a similar situation, only they were Spanish American.

My grandmother married a Mexican man and her sister married a Swede. They lived in different worlds after that and I've never met any of the Swedish clan. Anyway, *The Juice* was a fascinating read. . . .

> Georgia W. Babb, New Mexico

(Author's note: Rebecca Saletan was the editor of *The Sweeter the Juice.*)

Dear Mrs. Haizlip,

My reason for writing to you is to tell you that I have just read your book *The Sweeter the Juice,* borrowed from the Pinjarra Public Library.

There has obviously been much work and research gone into the writing of this book, but I want you to know how very much I have enjoyed it.

The story you had to tell was most interesting and the final chapter moved me to tears. You have been able to convey clearly to your readers just how you and your mother have felt. For some time I have kept a perpetual prayer list (said to be remembered by God after one dies) and I will place you and your family on my list.

Incidentally, my youngest grandson, who is fourteen, is quite dark-skinned, amongst a fair family—darker than an aboriginal boy in his class, and his colour darkens as the summer goes on. He was born with a white line, still there, which resembles a scar line from an operation, which reaches from central breast to his lower body. Who can tell the mystery of this colour. It is probably a throw back from generations past.

I hope that all the relatives you have traced remain close to you, and in particular I wish your dear mother well. I am a Yorkshire woman from England who has lived with my family here in Australia, for over twenty years.

Yours very sincerely,

Mrs. Jean Bryan, Australia

P.S. I am devoted to cats too.

Dear Mrs. Taylor Haizlip

After a two-day binge, I have completed your family's story. I must tell you, it goes beyond being superb.

My father, the seventh son in a family of sixteen children, never knew about his father's family, except for an uncle. Only my older aunts remember their grandmother when they were young. My father and I always planned to go to the archives to research his family. We constantly kept putting it off, and unfortunately he died six years ago. After reading your book, I plan to find my roots on both sides of my family.

Your discussion on race and color practically depicts a poem I wrote regarding my daughter. I constantly question when we can not only be accepted by "them," but by our own. We are the only race of people that keep trying to define ourselves.

My grandmother will be eighty in October, and she reminds me a lot of your mother. She too lost her mother at a young age. She had the stereotypical wicked stepmother as a young child, and was physically abused. To this day, she is afraid to talk about the pain. She told us if she kept the memories fresh, she would probably go crazy. Recently she relented and told me that she would be willing to record her life story. I cannot wait to hear it. Hopefully, releasing the pain, her demons will diminish. I have told her as children we cannot always determine what is done to us. We can only promise not to repeat the same with our own children. I must say, none of her eight children were abused. I have been writing stories and poems for a year, and would like to share another one. It is dedicated to my grandmother for her strength in a world that has not always been kind.

I could continue telling you about the pleasures I derived from *The Sweeter the Juice.* I am still extremely excited and will read it again before I pass it on to my mother. Please continue to write such enlightening stories. A sequel regarding what has transpired since you have found your family would be nice. . . .

You still seem to have unanswered questions. I believe sometimes we will never know the answer to the whys. A person's guilt can overwhelm them and they may not be able to pull themselves from under it.

Bye for now. I may write you again. SMILE. You have
been inspiration for me.

> With my best,
> Sherry White Talbert, Maryland

Dear Mrs. Haizlip,

While watching you on the *Oprah* show today, I remembered that I was not able to contact you by phone; which was
probably foreordained, because I would not be able to say on
the phone the things I could talk or write.

If I was a magician, I would wish I could whisk you to my
home on Sunday night when my gang is here; that would be
equal to a month of social studies.

My grandfather was a Morris (Dwight) but I never saw
him. He was evidently dead, and my grandmother (who was a
Moore and looked like any ole white woman). If she was or
not, I have no way of knowing, but she had brown children and
some light straight haired ones.

In my own gang (James Curtis Morris) three of my brothers in the West passed for something other than black Americans. They married one Mormon, at least two Mexicans and
they raised their umpteen children not black, but a few—like
four—years ago they became curious and started prying. We
have met four of them including one sister-in-law, and they
were as "happy as kings."

The one nephew is a big wig in the navy (as white); one
niece is in New Jersey, a lot are still in California, I guess.

At least six of the Illinois gang (which is where I was born)
are married to whites, including my youngest son, who has four
children.

I have four children, two girls in their sixties and two sons in their forties. When my second daughter was born in Chicago, the babies were brought to their mothers by "waiting mothers" who called the names. When I was called, the black girl who called it looked at me, called again, after my "here," she finally brought my very light golden-haired baby to me. My husband, her father, was quite brown.

He passed away in 1954, so I had to raise the two boys. Not alone, because of my daughters and their husbands. We were very successful. One has a good job in the steel plant. The other works for the state of Washington in the prison rehabilitation department. He travels here and there to put on workshops and is an interim pastor at a church near Tacoma where they live.

I am eighty-nine years and two months and six days old with a bad hip and leg and eyes, and a few other aches and pains. And a brain weak enough to think you could possibly be interested in this bunch of stuff I have written.

But I do a lot of miscellaneous writing to take up my spare time. And you look like a very nice person who would indulge an old lady in her last days.

So if you do read it, thank you very much.

> Your "Ohio cousin"
> Mrs. H. Mabel Walker, Ohio

Dear Mrs. Haizlip,

I have just finished reading *The Sweeter the Juice* and found your memoir to be outstanding in many ways. First, it provides this reader with insight into your fascinating family. Second, it reminds this reader of many of her own experiences. And third, it motivates this reader to continue with a genealogical search that is currently underway. Thank you, thank you, thank you.

Because of the unique experience I—a high school English teacher—had while reading your book, I feel that an apology must be expressed for writing to you in such a formal manner. However, my lack of a direct address made this impossible to do otherwise.

Somehow, I feel a spiritual bond that should permit me to post a handwritten note on my personal stationery, to refer to you by first name in the salutation and mine in the closing, and to share remembrances of things past in my life and dare to believe that you would find them interesting. This unique experience caused laughter about my double entrance as Miss Springtime in my six year old starring role in our school's spring extravaganza when I read about your role in the "DeCosta" pageant, sorrow about my paternal uncle who like your brother seemingly could not and/or would not bring honor to the family name, and fondness for parents who provided very well for their children. Yes, memories of Jack and Jill (My parents were charter members of the Raleigh NC Chapter), regular church attendance (Your Baptist minister father and my Methodist trustee father made sure of that) and AKA (I was presented in the 1959 Debutante Ball sponsored by Alpha Theta Omega Chapter but was too chicken to withstand the rigors of pledging at Morgan State University despite their invitation)—all seemingly substantiate this bond.

My own research began because of my desire as an only child to bring about some organization to memorabilia that I own and determine if there is a relationship between the families of Jurist James Iredell, Sr. who was appointed to the first U.S. Supreme Court by President George Washington and John Iredell who was my great grandfather and ancestor for whom my father was named.

I am slowly beginning to answer some very interesting questions. I am also looking into records of the Mitchiner family—my mother's family. Your book with its charts, photographs, bibliography in addition to the author's careful interweaving of historical facts, literary quotations and allusions, colorful descriptions, and delineated characters still leaves many unanswered and unanswerable questions.

Therefore, I shall indeed make more trips to the National Archives, Library of Congress, and selected university libraries as well; continue writing letters requesting documents to help fill in the gaps; and continue getting in touch with cousins to inquire about information that may have been shared with them. . . . By the way, the name of my great grandmother for whom I was named was Nancy Taylor Iredell. Her maiden name I only recently learned.

Again, thank you. . . .

> Sincerely yours,
> Mrs. Nancy Iredell Stroud, Maryland

Dear Shirlee Taylor Haizlip

I am so happy to have your book—made more special by your inscription. I found everything about it irresistible—the wonderful cover, the photographs which I still pore over and the engaging family history which reminds me so much of my own. Has there ever been a book I've enjoyed on so many levels? I don't think so! I found myself wondering if my grandmother, who lived in the Shaw section of Washington, D.C., as a teenager, bumped into your mother. If not, then surely my father's folks in Culpeper, Va., must have been at some summer do or lawn party with young Margaret. There were just so many parallels—not the least of which, my light skin and African identity and a life long fascination with perception and reality. Shirlee, I thoroughly enjoyed this book! and it still makes me think and remember and hear sounds in the streets where my grandparents walked with your grandparents.

> Sincerely,
> Sharon Dennis Wyeth, New Jersey

Dear Mrs. Haizlip,

After reading your book *The Sweeter the Juice,* I find that we both have some things in common, my great grandmother was white and Irish, my great grandfather was Cherokee Indian and it might be that my aunt by marriage is part of your family, the Virginia side. In the chapter of your Virginia side, some members of the Fortunes were mentioned, my aunt remembered John Fortune from Virginia. I sent her a list of names you mentioned in the Virginia chapter, and John was the only name she can remember, she also has Cherokee blood in her family . . .

I am also trying to trace my roots, my family came to Florida in 1859, and three generations are gone completely, we still have four generations left, but those that could remember anything of the past history are all gone. Thank you for allowing me to write this letter and all because of your book, please write more.

> Yours truly,
> Rufus J. Alexander, Jr., Florida

Dear Mrs. Hazlip,

I would like at some time to have an extended conversation with you about my family and background, as I feel yours has such similarities to mine. One of the powerful points, yet painful points, is that of my mother's having erased virtually all her connections to blackness, that is, to her family, and by extension of her children's connections to their family.

I have contacted my aunts, uncle and several cousins recently and have begun to rebuild my family ties after over thirty years. So far it has gone fairly well, some very good, some difficult. My friends have been unerringly supportive and loving. But it has given my mother a lot of pain and she fears that she will "have her life destroyed" by the truths of our hidden heritage, if her community should come to know it. Sadly, it has divided us to a degree—a lie that has yet again divided our family.

I hope to find someone to talk to about these matters, though my wife has listened intently, carefully and responsively. My closest friends live in other areas of the world.

Thanks for your help and consideration and thanks for your book. It has set me on a new and wholesome course.

Sincerely,

C. L., California

Dear Ms. Haizlip:

With a heavy heart I read the last page of your book; I couldn't believe it was over. Your history was fascinating, although I kept referring to the pictures so often I was ready to rip them out just to keep them near.

I think the reason for my near-obsession with this subject matter is a desire to know *my* roots. Ours was a clouded past. My paternal grandmother made the following reference sixty years ago when speaking to her "new daughter-in-law" (my mother): "Francis (my father) *did* tell that his family was well, er, Portuguese?"

We suspect that there was more to the story—like they were Portuguese *black*. My British mother knew her husband was dark (Spanish) from his father's side, but not much was known about the ethnicity of his mother. There was a grandmother named Tennessee Camden, but that's about all we know.

Then my mother began searching for *her* past. Her birth-father in England had never seen her and everyone considered him the "black sheep" of the family. Someone said he was descended from the Moors. My grandmother referred to a mysterious cousin named "Helen Elijah."

In 1963 my mother and I went over to England to look for her father and found out he had died in 1947. She did manage to see a dime-size faded grey photo of his face. When I saw it, I remember seeing a friendly face with a broad nose and very "kinky" hair. At last my mother knew where her unmanageable, coarse, despised (at that time) hair came from. Perhaps that would also explain our Keloid scarring.

My mother did mention something which in retrospect seems unusual: she vividly remembers being terrified of Ku Klux Klanners when she lived in Rhode Island in the 1920's. She said they threatened *her* house. At any rate, none of this was important to me as I grew up in our middle class white/Hispanic/Oriental neighborhood in Long Beach. When I was young we had to fill out "Federal Survey Cards" which asked our race. My father told me to put "Hispanic."

For years, however, I have felt something—I don't know if it was a "kinship" since I grew up surrounded by whiteness—for black Americans. My sister has also felt a similar desire to know "what" we are. All the "players" who could tell us are dead: my mother died nearly 30 years ago, along with grandparents, aunts, uncles and our father. My only sister's daughter was born 27 years ago with a serious congenital eye malady.

The possibility has been suggested that at least one of our relatives was a black Albino. One of *my* daughters (the other is a baby, so we don't know about her yet) and one of my sister's sons has what our kids call "Brillo Pad hair." My hair is somewhat coarse and when I was teaching in a Santa Ana school seventeen years ago, one of my close friends, a black teacher came up to me, examined my hair closely, and said (really, *she* said this—not me), "Girl, there be a nigger in *your* woodpile somewhere." She was also a hairdresser, and began trimming my hair because no one in the white salons could do it correctly. Incidentally, please be assured that those were her words, not mine. We were brought up in a "proper" household which would never tolerate racial epithets.

You probably receive thousands of letters like this, but thank you for taking the time to read this one. Your book has offered me the chance to speculate about my past. Thank you again for your thought-provoking book. . . .

        Sincerely,
        Vicki Surges, Nevada

P.S. My stepmother threw out most of the old family pictures, but I've enclosed a copy of one taken in 1953. At that time my parents' marriage was considered a "mixed" marriage.

Dear Ms. Haizlip:

I want you to know how much I enjoyed your book *The Sweeter the Juice.* I recently finished reading it and have spent the time since recommending it to everyone I know and a few people I don't! Your openness and candor not only about your family's history, but your feelings about that history and its influence on you were moving.

I was struck, however, by your statement about the history of Africans in Portugal. You stated you were told that all Africans were driven from Portugal in, I believe you said, the 11th century. Whoever told you this must have been engaging in the same kind of denial as the couple who decided someone could not be the husband's ancestor, despite the correct name, address and date of birth, because the man was black. As much as it pains most Portuguese to admit it, there are few who do not have African ancestry.

In the mid-1400s Portugal's Prince Henry the Navigator first captured Africans while exploring the west coast of Africa.

By the middle of the 1500s, Portugal was bringing Africans to Portugal on a regular basis as laborers. There was, however, no prohibition on marriage between the Portuguese and the Africans and intermarriage was common. According to many historians, for a time there were more Africans in parts of Portugal than Portuguese.

This mingling of Portuguese and African blood and cultures is no where more evident than in the Cape Verde Islands, formerly part of Portugal and now an independent nation. Somewhere between the history of mainland Portugal and Cape Verde is the history of the Azores, the islands from which my family comes. Few Portuguese, especially those from the southern part of the mainland and either of the archipelagos mentioned are without African blood.

In my own family I have seen photos of those in my mother's generation in whose faces our African ancestry is clearly visible. No matter, that generation would rather die than admit we are racially mixed. My cousins and I, who take pride in our African heritage, simply do not discuss the matter with those of the previous generation; it would effect no change in attitudes. I suspect the person who told you there were no Africans in Portugal after the eleventh century was, like much of my family, fearful he might have to accept his own history.

Sincerely,
Arlene Joy Mitchell, Texas

Dear Shirlee Taylor Haizlip,

I enjoyed your book *The Sweeter the Juice* and I enjoyed you and your husband on the *Oprah* show.

I know a lot about the Black Portuguese because I am one.

Back in Isabella's and Ferdinand's time the Jews and the Moslems were evacuated from Spain and Portugal. . . . not the

Blacks. It was because of religion and not skin color because by then, with all the exploring by the Portuguese, there were plenty of Black, Japanese and Chinese brides living in Portugal.

The Portuguese have a lot to be proud of although we get very little credit. They do not discriminate against other nationalities. They are really very sweet people.

I saw a good example of it when I was on a train from Spain into Portugal on my way to Lisbon.

Some Spanish tend to be arrogant and the conductors on that train were a prime example. When we came to the border and the Spanish conductors got off and the Portuguese came on to take their places, the atmosphere in the train changed!

There are a lot of Black Portuguese. Africans who live in Portuguese places as the former Mozambique and the Cape Verde Islands. It is a national thing . . . and mixed marriages as well.

I am the youngest of nine and the only one still alive. I am seventy-seven. In the past several years I have been looking up my own genealogy and discovered that some names are Spanish, Portuguese, French, Dutch and Jewish. I am delighted. I always felt that being just Portuguese was boring as so many of my classmates in grammar school were combinations of other nationalities! I have a picture of my father's father and he looks just like Sitting Bull . . . and the Portuguese were here before Columbus and traded with them and no doubt married! I think all this is God's little joke on humanity. He does have a wonderful sense of humor. I think each and every one of us has a bit of everything.

Incidentally, I always thought that my oldest brother looked like the Indian on the nickel. Years later at my brother's funeral, his son, in the funeral car, said "I always thought that my father looked like the Indian on the nickel." We lived miles apart and I had never mentioned it to anyone.

Ema Gil Wykes, Massachusetts

Dear Soror and Link Sister Shirlee,

While reading your book review in the *Detroit Free Press* last month, I immediately felt a kinship with you. However after reading your book, I had an overwhelming desire to communicate with you as well.

I too am an AKA and was inducted as a charter member into the Great Lakes Chapter of the Links. . . . My children were in Jack and Jill, Inc. and my mother shares my same affiliations, plus others. Perhaps the most significant similarity though between you and us, is that my mother and I are MORRIS descendants. Like you, I am addicted to genealogy and am tireless regarding the search for my ancestors. I've been hooked for about six months and decided to begin with my deceased father's side of the family since less is known. They are Conleys, Tysons, Bingas, and Hughes'.

My Morris descendants are from Canada and are registered as an "historic family" in the Buxton Museum of Raleigh Township, Ontario. Their family trees were prepared by the descendants who live in the Buxton settlement. Nevertheless, I plan to gather census data on my own to verify what is listed.

I believe that the information about the Morris family before they came to Canada is based on oral history and perhaps, some speculation. As far as I know, no pre-Canadian census information has been gathered on the Canadian Morrises. The story has been told that the Morris family were never enslaved and settled in Connecticut and Vermont before coming to Canada. Yet, as a Black family of fair complexion no one can answer how and where they originated.

Like your Morrises, this Canadian family was for the most part very, very fair. My grandmother and all but one of her siblings could pass for white. As a child forty-plus years ago, my grandmother, Barbara Grace Morris Greenidge, would take me on downtown shopping trips and strangers would comment on her perceived altruism. "How nice of you to take your maid's daughter shopping with you."

My grandmother's sister Kate was the only sibling with any significant color. She had a deep egg nog complexion. Most had "dead straight" hair, the kind that defies permanent waving. Also, my grandmother's brother Jim married white and decided to pass for white after his marriage (see picture). They disappeared. Like you, I too have wondered when I look at white faces, could they be relatives.

My grandmother, Barbara Grace Morris was born in 1893 in Merlin Township, Ontario. She married Robert Greenidge a physician from the former British West Indies who had a dark brown complexion. James Morris is the family patriarch. He too had an Irish mother. . . . We know that his father, George Hatter, had been a mulatto (fugitive) slave from Virginia or West Virginia before coming to Canada. . . . I've enclosed some photos of Morris descendants and some written information.

I would be remiss if I did not thank you for truly revealing your self and your family among the pages. I laughed and I cried, but most of all, it validated my right to wonder and even to discuss my multiethnicities. Like you, I am proud to be a Black American, but why should that mean I have to deny what is not Black. As we both know, most Black Americans descend from at least one white relative, yet, many Blacks are offended when one discusses anything but one's blackness. You have announced, "It's OK." You are a trailblazer. Thanks for leaving your mark.

Sisterly and God bless you,
Barbara Hughes Allen Smith, Ph.D.,
Michigan

Dear Ms. Haizlip,

I read your book *The Sweeter the Juice* this summer and I cannot tell you what a profound effect it has on me.

Our lives seem to have several parallels. My father was born of mixed parentage, and as a "Red Bone" I have faced several conflicts as well. Although to my knowledge no one from our family "passed," I always felt alienated by both races. I have always been fiercely proud of my black heritage, but learned early in life there would always be some "sister" and "brothers" that would never fully accept me into what I felt and still feel is my birth right.

It has taken me many years to come to terms with this alienation I have sometimes felt from my own people but finally came to realize that what is most important is that I know who I am and from whence I have come. Your book and your mother's courage have reaffirmed that belief.

I was also fascinated by the fact that you grew up in Ansonia, the town of my father's birth. My grandfather migrated from Virginia to Connecticut as a young boy of 14. He settled in Ansonia (his name was Solomon Walker). He had four sons, Solomon (Sol), Johnnie, Albert, and my father Ralph. I don't known if your parents knew any of them but Ansonia was and probably still is a small town. My sisters and brothers and I grew up in New Haven—all of us being WWII babies. . . .

I applaud you for your determination to find your mother's past—what a beautiful gift for a daughter to give to a mother.

Sincerely and with much admiration,
Cleo (Penny) Walker Saffoe, North Carolina

Dear Shirlee,

I just finished your book *The Sweeter the Juice.* I saw you recently on the *Oprah* show. . . . My interest in your book probably won't come to any surprise. I was adopted at infancy.

My birthparents were military brats both stationed in Germany in the early 60's. My mother had flaming red hair and skin as white as snow while my father was a mixture of Native American and black. His father was a lieutenant colonel which was rare back then. According to my birth mother, her father who was only ranked a Captain and had to answer to the Colonel, couldn't stand the fact that he was outranked by a "nigger." It didn't stop my birthparents love for each other tho, and they kept their love for each other a secret for two years until my birthfather's family got orders to return to the states. My birth mother was fifteen, pregnant and devastated.

They kept in touch by letter and she hid the pregnancy for six months until it could no longer be hidden. At first my birthmother told her father that she had gotten pregnant by a white GI who was on R&R, until a letter from my birth father was intercepted by the chaperone at her high school and handed over to her father.

Her father, who had originally said he'd help raise the child, changed his mind quickly when he discovered who had really gotten her pregnant. He held a pistol to her head and said, "You're not raising a nigger baby in this family." In less than two weeks she was shipped off to stay with an Aunt and to serve part of that time at a home for unwed mothers in Oklahoma City.

The pain of the situation, the helplessness of her mother controlled by an abusive husband and the loneliness she experienced was unexplainable and she gave birth to me all alone on February 4th, 1963. Some of the other girls in the home told her that if she looked at her baby, the face would haunt her forever, so she only asked the sex.

I was adopted two weeks later by a white family. They were told that the mother was Irish and the father was Puerto Rican. They were chosen to adopt me mainly because my older sister, also adopted was of Spanish origin and they thought the match was good.

So all my life I grew up in a very white middle class family. I had a great childhood and my parents were so wonderful, but I knew someday I would search for my roots. The day I turned eighteen I dragged a friend down to the adoption agency, thinking I'd be given my file with all the answers of my past. No such luck.

This began my twelve-year search for who Wendy really was. I always knew I had black in me. I just knew. I had wavy brown hair and olive skin and green eyes. People always said I looked exotic with my color and high cheekbones. For almost fifteen years of my life I have straightened my hair. Ha. Not anymore.

In 1992 I paid an underground searcher $2500 to find my birth mother after every door was closed in my face. Within two months they had found her. She was living in Virginia. Why had I known she'd be so far away? Although my first call to her was a tough one, we have since become like best friends. I had opened the floodgates to her past that she had buried for thirty years.

For the first year of knowing her it was strained. I had relocated my husband, three children and myself all the way from California to Virginia to get to know her. My husband being a native Californian hated it there and we came back after only nine months. She felt like she had lost me again.

My biggest problem with Sally then was that every time I asked her about my birth father she would change the subject. I backed off and figured it was very painful for her to remember him. To this day, he is the only man she ever loved. Eventually, I decided against her will to find him myself. My relationship with Sally came to an end the day I found him on June 11, 1993.

With the tidbits of info she had shared with me, I wrote an organization called Overseas Brats and they put me in touch with the head of the alumni of the high school my father had attended in Germany. I wrote this person a letter detailing all I knew about my father and got a call back from the guy saying he had gone to school with him. Would you believe the first thing he asked me was, "What do you look like?" I was pissed. I mean, did it really matter?

He finally told me his name and gave me his phone number. My birthfather lives in Mashpee, Massachusetts on Cape Cod. Once again, I couldn't believe that my birthfather also lived on the East Coast. I called him that same day, petrified. He was friendly but cautious and told me he hoped we could meet someday. I hung up feeling as tho he didn't really care but before I knew it the phones were ringing off the hook with newfound relatives calling. I was so happy.

In late June of 1993 I flew to Massachusetts to meet my birth father and paternal grandparents and family for the first time. By this time we had both exchanged pictures and were very excited to meet. My father wrote me a letter saying I was the picture he had always known I'd look like. What did that mean? I was his light skinned baby, his white daughter?

If I didn't know my father and passed him on the street I'd think he was hispanic. His father was said to be white and black mixture and Pennsylvania Dutch. He had beautiful blue eyes. His mother is Wampanoag Indian from Mashpee.

All this was hard to piece together in such a short visit. A lot of the family looked all black to me with light skin. The girls were beautiful. One of my father's brothers had blonde hair. It was weird to see such a marination of hues.

In all the excitement, I realized why my birth mother kept her silence about his identity. In youth only love mattered, but in time her father's constant psychological abuse of how she screwed a nigger and gave birth to one had taken its toll on her and she was scared.

To make a difficult story short (and I could go on and on, HA) the moral is that after 32 years of life, I know who I am. When I have to check off one of those stupid boxes of what my race is, I check "other." Because I am a mixture of many things. And I love all races.

We all live within our exterior shells just like everyone else and I believe it's our souls that make us who we really are. And I'm happy to report that after six months of silence with my birth mother, I called her to see if we could mend our wounds. We did and we are back to being close friends again.

Last year for my birthday I flew back East to Virginia and from there we drove to Alexandria where we picked up my father at the airport. My birth parents hadn't seen each other for over 30 years. They kissed and embraced and I, their baby girl cried tears of joy. This was what life was supposed to be, but because of skin tone it never came to be. It was a happy moment but a sad one too. Their misfortune was another loving couple's fortune and my life was ultimately changed. We didn't have a choice.

Thanks Shirlee for sharing your story too. I've often wanted to put mine in print not for money or recognition but just to give hope to others who might be searching. Your book is about hope and survival. I think the more family we have, the more there is to love. . . .

> Sincerely and God Bless You,
> Wendy Quinn, California

To: Shirlee
From: Donna Iwagaki

Dorothy Walden is an eighty-six-year-old bright woman that has just suffered two strokes. Her daughter and I were co-workers and her granddaughter is in Tokyo studying with a Georgetown program.

Dorothy's father Papa Harris was a Superintendent of Negro Schools in Meridian, Mississippi. Dorothy wanted all Negro women to learn stenography skills and they set up their own school, bought the books and typewriters and equipment. There is a wonderful rich history to her story and reading your life just gives me gooseflesh with awe.

During WWII Dorothy applied for a federal job at the Treasury department and tells this wonderful story of how proudly she wrote Negro across the top of her application. How all the other office workers slipped around the corner to look at her. Her daughter also tells the story that her bosses would ask Dorothy to go to Helfts and shop for their wives. I didn't realize that if you were African American and tried something on in the store you bought it. There are so many rich wonderful histories to be found.

Thanks ever so much.
Donna Iwagaki, California

Whiteness on My Mind

Dear Mrs. Haizlip,
"Gram, we got this kinky hair from someplace." My wife remembers her cousin making that remark to the cousin's

grandmother many years ago. My wife's maternal grandmother, sister to the aforementioned Gram also had tight curls and otherwise carried a close family resemblance. At this point, we still don't know where, or more properly, who that someplace was, but reading *The Sweeter the Juice* has aroused my interest in finding out.

As I read through the last chapter and the Epilogue, I had to wipe away the tears streaming down my face in order to discern the words on the page. I have not been so moved by a book in a long time. I happened to catch a small bit of your family's TV appearance and when the familiar title showed up at the public library last week, I was able to read your story. I don't usually cry when I read books, but your recounting of the coming together of your family apparently cracked the crust of cynicism that I have been accumulating of late.

About twenty-eight years ago, after five sons born to us, my wife and I began the proceedings which eventually led to the adoption of two daughters of mixed race. Since that time we have enjoyed observing people and speculating on their possible racial background. Just as you tell of looking for clues in the features of those you met as you sought out your relatives, we notice hair and noses and the subtle shading of fingernails as we wonder if we are seeing a new kin of our daughters.

With the news filled with stories of ethnic strife around the world, and neo-nazi skinheads making the headlines here at home, your cousin Jeff's positive reaction to your revelations about his background really gave me a lift. Best wishes for your continued success and happiness. We hope that you will accept us as a couple more of:

Your Cousins,

Jess and Mary Lu Strack, Illinois

Dear Mrs. Haizlip,

This is a shameless fan letter and I have never written one of these before but I bought your book yesterday and am so enthralled with the story and with the power of the issues you so gracefully describe — I had to write to you to say thank you.

I teach a course primarily for teachers called Child, Family and Community. My goal in this class is to enable the students to look at themselves and their own families before they go out to work with other people's children. Indirectly I have heard versions of your story dozens of times as the students put together their genograms. But I have never had any resources which spelled out the black/white experience so eloquently. I am going to use your story as a text; an example of what careful scholarship can reap about one's past, and an overview of American racial history.

I do not mean to gush on but once more, thank you. I am off to recommend your book to my friends.

> Sincerely,
> Deborah Davis,
> Professor of Child Development, California

Dear Shirlee Taylor Haizlip,

I have just completed your book *The Sweeter the Juice* and I am full of questions. I was full of questions before and that is why I read the book. It was excellent. I read it in five days. I hope I do not offend you in any way. I have been very interested in the black culture. I have been reading a lot to answer my questions. Toni Morrison is one of my favorite authors and I have just finished *Black Boy,* by Richard Wright, and *Black like Me,* by John Howard Griffin.

I am a white person although I don't know what that means. My ancestors can be traced back to England and I was raised in white culture. While reading the book I was frequently reminded of the phrase ". . . And denied the black soil from which this rhythm was born" from *Jelly's Last Jam*. That is my all-time favorite musical. The music just goes way down deep into me where I can feel it from my head down to my toes and it takes me to another world. I found it ironic how you too saw the connection from your story to the musical and mentioned it in the book.

I looked on my CD case and saw your daughter's name. I saw the traveling show in Chicago so I do not know if I saw her dance or not. I remember; when I saw the musical I kept wishing I was black so that I could sing and dance like that. That was an incorrect statement assuming that all black people can sing and dance like that. Assuming things is something I do too much of.

I am having trouble understanding what it means to say one is black or one is white. Isn't Grace, a white woman, just as black as your mother? And isn't your mother, a black woman, just as white as Grace? How much "black blood" is needed to make someone black or white? And what does a person's actual skin color mean? The way I understand it is that it is more of a culture rather than a blood percentage.

One thing I remember in *Black like Me* was a statement he made about how white people never think about race and black people always do. Actually that same idea was mentioned on *ER* a few months ago too. I think that may be accurate.

Another thing that I wondered about was how it seemed that you favored people who were darker. For example, your husband and your father. Why is the black culture more favored than the white one? What if you or a family member married a very white skinned person? How could that be looked upon?

I understand that there are two separate worlds, a black one and a white one. I don't understand why though? Where do Asians fit in? I appreciate different cultures and I love to learn about new ones. But I don't understand why everyone doesn't welcome and celebrate the differences as one human race. I don't understand why your family is still a white part and a black part. What does that mean?

It seems the more I read, the more I want to know. Do you know any books that you can recommend for me to read? I will never know what it is like to be a black person. I live in a very white world. Sometimes I think a very dumb white world.

I live in a black neighborhood for the summer. And I watch the other culture and it just seems to make more sense than my world sometimes. Sometimes I look down at my very white arms and I think that my peach skin isn't very attractive. Many of our ideas and values are pretty odd and our music just doesn't have any meaning and feel to it. I am running on a tangent, which I will stop now.

There are just so many things in this world that I just don't understand. And I read and search for answers but sometimes I don't think there are any answers. Maybe part of understanding is understanding that we can't understand it all. Please write me back with any comments or answers. I appreciate anything you think. Thank you very much for your time.

Sincerely,

Lynette Workman, Illinois

Shirley Taylor Haizlip,

I just finished reading your book, and really have reflected and thought a lot about my own and my society's perceptions, values, assumptions. I see the strengths and shadows in myself and all of us. Thank you for bringing your family and experiences to me.

Anne Fege, California

Dear Friend,

Thank you for your strength and direction to bring us all closer to love. I really appreciate the "shift in consciousness" you gave me — understanding is so precious to open the heart.

Sincerely,

James Piver, California

Dear Mrs. Haizlip:

I read the fine review of your book in the *Los Angeles Times* and found it in my local bookstore last weekend.

Just completed the chapter on your father, Rev. Julian Taylor, which I read with tears in my eyes. Your pride in him and in your family rings through the book. It reads like a novel and I am truly moved by it.

As a long-term "American" I believe firmly your theory that if we would all accept how racially mixed we all are — maybe we could all recognize each other as struggling human beings. Langston Hughes was right! Varying shades of beige will be better!

A similar "secret" seems to exist in my family. My mother was a very fair skinned redhead who married a very dark-skinned, wavy-haired man. All of us looked like our Mom, but I always wondered at my father's difference from his own family of fair skin and dark-haired individuals. Both sides of the family came from the South (Oklahoma, Kentucky, and Tennessee). My paternal aunt discounts any "mixed" blood as she does her genealogies of the paternal "English" side. However, my father always said there was Cherokee blood, which my great-uncle told him about. My friend (half-Cherokee) said when she saw family pictures, "Your father looks like a full-blood Cherokee, where was his family from?" HMMM! Your excellent book has whetted my curiosity about denial in my own family and my own father's sense of "less than" in a color based family and society.

Just wanted to share that with you and let you know how I am enjoying your story. Your family must be very proud of you. Somewhere I know, Margaret feels better about herself and what happened to her. May many read it—it's a necessary and thought-provoking book.

Most sincerely,
Patricia E. Watson, California

Dear Ms. Haizlip:

I have just finished reading your book, *The Sweeter the Juice.*

I very much enjoyed the book and admired your courage in discussing your family's history and your personal journey to identify family members. Unfortunately, we are schizophrenic when it comes to race.

Your book caused me to reexamine my attitudes and prejudices concerning race. In recent years, I have represented the City of New Haven, Connecticut on environmental matters and was able to recognize many of the landmarks and towns in Connecticut described in your book. Similarly, having lived in Washington, D.C. for the last 11 years, I very much appreciated your vivid description of Washington from 1850 to the middle of the 20th century.

I hope I will have the honor of meeting you one day. Many thanks for your book.

Sincerely,

Benjamin F. Wilson, Washington, D.C.

Dear Ms. Haizlip,

After reading about you in *American Heritage,* I promptly read your book *The Sweeter the Juice.* My heritage is Italian-American, my parents born here of immigrant mother and father. My husband is mostly Welsh-American with English on his mother's side. Together we produced six children, three boys and three girls—all of them with very crinkly, coarse, wiry hair. My husband has the same hair. We have joked about it through the years and yes, the girls still lament about their "hard to manage" hair.

Never did we dream of any black connections until I read your book. Even then I had not yet heard that "nigger Tanner" was a name given to my husband's maternal grandmother who was of English heritage. (This was a recent disclosure.)

Looking at this great-grandmother's family portrait there you see her parents and four siblings. Three of the siblings including great-grandmother have blonde fuzzy, crinkly coarse hair. It is very apparent in the photograph.

I devoured all your meaningful remarks in the book. It was poignant and I so admired your zeal in finding your mother's sister. Now I am about to do a family search on great grand-mother Amelia Wilbur of upstate New York.

My question is a genetic one: is crinkly, coarse, wiry hair found in all kinds of humans or is it an indication of black heritage? As you wrote, most of us white Americans have black connections it is so logical. The gene seems to *be so strong* that among our eleven grandchildren, seven of them have the crinkly, coarse, wiry hair. Are you smiling? I wanted to share all this with you. Your book was marvelous. Thanks for listening. Hearing from you would be wonderful.

Sincerely,

Bess Jones, New York

Dear Ms. Haizlip

I picked up *The Sweeter the Juice* and was not able to put it down until I was finished. It is still beside my desk, where I will read it again before my husband gets it. Thanks for writing it.

I am a photograph historian; I've just finished a book on the history of photography in Alabama—it is out in the world seeking an academic publisher—and have a book on dating/identifying family photographs researched and outlined. I was fascinated by your photographs and the way you wrote about them.

Looking at the photographs before I read the book, I noted that M. M. Morris looks very conflicted—untidy hair with uptight jacket and blouse—she looks as if she is holding her mouth tight but may explode from the pressure. Wm. Morris Sr. looks away from the camera (is this a detail from a group photo?) in a way that seemed to me prophetic and seems more so after reading about him.

I found your book painful and uplifting to read. Painful because the problems of flawed perceptions you raise seem to me as intractable as those in Greek tragedies, and uplifting because you don't gloss them over, or put them behind, but are brave enough to leave them out on the table. I don't know what can heal our nation's pathology of race, but I can say from my own family (white, mostly poor until my parents' generation) that there is a pathology of defeat, guilt, and blame that must be both acknowledged and put aside if this sickness is ever to heal.

I want to tell you a story that resonates in curious ways against your own; rendering the issues of perceptions, race, and culture very complicated indeed. Last week, I was in a small old Alabama town. My hostess had once contacted me to obtain a copy of a photograph of her ancestors (he an antebellum surveyor/landowner/slave-owner.)

I had copied the photograph at the home (in another town) of a gently raised, well-off 100 year old lady (mixed race, black by culture), whiter and much less work-worn than my grandmother. She told me her story of the white slave-owner, his two families black and white, and his bequest of cotton lands to every child (three "black" three "white"). The surveyor arranged the marriage of the black mother to his white overseer.

A sister of the centenarian married a Jew, moved away, and passed for white (she thought that her sister marrying a Jew was odder than her marrying a white). She seemed comfortable in black culture, yet accepting of her white background. She was more attached to the surveyor's memory than to that of the overseer, feeling that there was an emotional bond between the surveyor and her black ancestor (confirmed by his legacy to his mixed-blood children) that she did not sense so strongly in the next generation.

The centenarian was given the photograph of her white great-grandfather by his white grandson's wife, who said that she most closely resembled him (I wonder if the wife was disturbed by the image and wanted to rid her family of it). She said that I could have a copy made for the other lady and that I could recount her personal history if the other lady was interested.

My recent hostess found the details convincing and disturbing. When I left her, she seemed, having wanted to hear all, to want to bury this new history behind a cool facade, but I believe that she will be haunted by it. I am persuaded that, in relation to the issues that concern you, there are infinite variations: each family has its own distinctive pattern of loss, of difficulty, and occasionally of salvage and new life.

Your book has cast the above history (and my own) into new perspective. I am richer (though more troubled) for your book. Thank you for writing the story of your quest. I hope that you and your family will find renewed strength and wisdom from it, and that it will give you peace (but not such peace that you quit writing).

> Sincerely,
> Frances Osborn Robb, Alabama

Dear Shirlee,

I just finished your book *The Sweeter the Juice* and wanted to let you know that I was thoroughly intrigued by your family's story, and your search for the truth. I hope you have stayed in touch with your newfound family members. I was especially excited by the fact that your great uncle Edward had lived in Buffalo on Elmwood Avenue (by any odd chance #1032!) for I lived there in a sprawling apartment house when I was a teen!

My sister has been tracing our family tree and located Indian in our bloodline, which we'd always been told about and never tried to keep hidden.

Another sister could have no children of her own and adopted a set of twin boys, and a black (Mulatto) girl. None have attempted to locate their birth parents as yet. The girl is 23 now and still at home, and definitely is dark, but dates only white men/boys. (So far anyway!) She faced some of the problems expected considering the white society she grew up in, but my sister would not stand for anyone putting her down. This sister was also instrumental in forming my own opinions about colored people, as she is twelve years older than I and has many black friends. I do too, and have had them to my home.

My mother has had her share of a bad beginning in life — taken from her own mother at age four and not seeing her again til she was eighteen. What tales she's told me! I've been considering trying to write myself. So many stories in my head that some may find interesting enough to read. I only wish there were more hours in a day.

My mother is seventy-eight, and in July we're flying up to Buffalo to visit my oldest sister and catching up on family there, as well as visit old stomping grounds of Mom's. Now I'll be able to put faces and pictures to the people and places she talks about so often.

Take care and God Bless,
     Sincerely,
     M.R., Florida

Dear Ms. Haizlip:

After seeing you on *Oprah*, I thought perhaps you could give me some genealogical advice. My family is predominantly white, with some Cherokee heritage also. There has been some speculation through the years that we also have black relatives.

Going backwards though the generations, my family has roots in Oklahoma, Texas, Tennessee, Kentucky, the Carolinas, and Virginia. I have done some genealogical research, and I have discovered that there was at least one family, in Kentucky, that had a number of slaves.

Since I was a child, I have always been interested in the black cowboy and rodeo star, Bill Pickett. His family came from Oklahoma and Texas like mine, he was also part white and Cherokee, we shared the same last name, and in fact, my father's name is also Bill Pickett. I have read some information about him, but I have never learned much more about his background than the above information. I have no idea if our two families are related, but I've always wanted to research the subject.

Sincerely,

E.P.H., Oklahoma

Dear Shirlee,

I just finished reading your book *The Sweeter the Juice* and enjoyed it very much.

I felt sad for your mother. Nothing can ever take the place of a loving family when you are growing up. Black and white people with prejudiced views never know the joys of learning more about God's great creations. They miss out on so much when they let preconceived ideas prevent them from looking into another culture. For some, like your mother's family, they feel they must choose the black or white race. They never see the possibility of enjoying both.

Prejudice can cause so much hatred, sorrow, bitterness and especially for those like your mother, so much loneliness.

In the South there is still much underlying prejudice (some not so underlying).

There is peace in knowing that the Bible says God is not partial (Acts 10:34, 35) but loves all those that exercise love toward him.

In reading about your life, I think of you as a friend.

Sincerely,

Carole

Dear Ms. Haizlip:

Please add me to your list of admirers. Thanks to our high school Latin and French teacher, Betty Keat, I read *The Sweeter the Juice.* While I won't get on a soapbox, I am urging people to read your book: my daughter, who teaches in a well integrated, but still segregated school; my co-workers; family members and chance acquaintances.

Educated at Hunter College junior high and high school and receiving a B.A. and M.A. from Hunter College (with six years of Latin, incidentally), I was exposed to a fairly good mix of colors and personalities. However, I came from an all-white (at the time) neighborhood in the Bronx, and after marrying and facing the costs of private schools for our children in New York City, moved to this very white suburb. Your book has helped me revisit people and locales from my childhood and it has put many things back into perspective.

Your description of the "delicious" skin colors on page 30 was poetry—I loved it. Thanks for the opportunity to visit your homes and those of your relatives and for your vivid descriptions of furnishings.

The section about an eccentric relative who copied and constructed fashionable clothes for family members reminded me of things my mother did. She would copy Grace Kelly's styles from the movies—she also used upholstery fabric (which was cut wider and thus used less yardage) for some of my dresses!

Since it did not pertain to your topic, it was not mentioned in your book—but I wonder about the resentment held by some black women (with whom I worked in the sixties) toward mixed marriages, especially that of successful black men to white women. Has that changed at all? Thank you for *The Sweeter the Juice.* It truly delighted and instructed.

Sincerely,
Helen S. Gardner, New Jersey

Dear Mrs. Haizlip:

There is a possibility that you might remember me but on the other hand you might not know me at all. I lived most of my young life in Ansonia, that is from age 3–26. I was raised by my maternal grandparents who lived in a large yellow apartment house at 88 Howard Avenue, which was on the hill overlooking the river, the mills and part of the street on which stood your father's church and parsonage.

We lived in the first floor owner's apartment in the house and rented out the four apartments above our living quarters. My grandparents owned the building and my grandfather Wiliam Toras worked as a butcher at Brown's Market which was located directly over the bridge from your father's church.

I just learned of your book when I read the review in *The New York Times* and although the review did not mention Ansonia, I knew immediately what small town you were writing about. I read it in two sittings. It is a fascinating, warm and very eye-opening book.

Growing up in the white community of Ansonia, I never realized until I read your book how circumscribed by unwritten rules our lives were. I for one had no black friends until I entered high school and then only my teammates on the football team and a few black girls from my high school classes. I also didn't realize that despite the fact that you lived in a northern town, your lives were more circumscribed than mine. Your stories about leisure time and vacations in a segregated society were most interesting.

I do remember your mother and father. Your father I remember more vividly because I used to see him about town and what most impressed me was that he carried himself with great dignity and was always impeccably dressed. He had an aura about him and oh how I envied his automobiles!! I met your mother only once and that was during the 1950 Census when she called at our home and sat in our kitchen enumerating our family. It's really too bad that the invisible barriers were so high and unscalable that the people of Ansonia could not get to know each other better.

Yours is a wonderful, wonderful book and account of your family and your search for your white ancestors. Research-wise, I know what you went through because during my 30 year U.S. government career I spent 15 of them at the National Archives assisting researchers like you. I hope your book goes a long way toward destroying the myth that any segment of our society is racially pure. Keep up the good work and go out there and lecture and teach so that the myth will be destroyed.

Sincerely yours,
Walter Barbash, Virginia

P.S. I know your sister Jewelle from AHS drama club. I believe she was a year or two behind me.

Dear Shirley:

I just finished reading *The Sweeter the Juice* and feel compelled to write you and thank you for that book. I work at Oakwood School and heard you speak at the Library Tribute we had at the Universal Hilton. In fact you happily signed my book after learning my name was Melissa.

Your book gives every person cause to question their family's roots but having two sets of grandparents who are from the south (who trace their roots back to plantations and the DAR), I had to chuckle to myself thinking about the distinct possibility of an African American lurking in their genes (not to mention the one they are facing in their future).

I am engaged to an African American man (Michael). Needless to say, one set of grandparents is horrified at my decision to marry this amazing guy. I would love to have them read your book to understand the complexities and possibilities of this country's racial legacy, not to mention their own.

While I will never fully comprehend what it means to be Black in this country, your book painted a vivid picture of your family's experience that will leave an indelible mark on the way I consider my fiancé and his family's experience and all of the other Black people I know and will meet in the future.

I realize that your book can only speak to your experience and not for all people, but I recognized many common threads between your experience and my fiancé and his family's experience. I am giving my future mother in law your book this weekend as I know she will be fascinated by it.

I am sure the children Michael and I plan to have will have questions about their mixed heritage but I am enchanted and encouraged at your notion that your "roots grow in many gardens." Perhaps they will understand that one day too.

I am in love with the idea of those varied roots and want my children to experience all of them. I hope that they will never be faced with having to hide parts of their heritage in order to have job opportunities or to live in a better neighborhood—but I guess anything is possible when you stop to consider the racism that exists the world over and the snap judgments people make about skin color.

This has been a lengthy diatribe about my life, but it's my way of expressing how much you have caused me to think and how much I appreciated you story. I'm in a Masters in Psychology program at Pepperdine at night and am taking cross-cultural counseling this semester from a wonderful man named Dr. Daryl Rowe. He likes to say that his skin is "rich in hue" and has "lots of melanin in it." My class, needless to say, is twenty white women, one Asian woman and one white man—

Dr. Rowe has a lot to teach us about many cultures but I am particularly interested in learning about his own and telling him about your book.

                    Warm regards,
                    M.P., California

P.S. I noticed *Jelly's Last Jam* is coming to Pasadena for a short time—is Melissa in that one too?

Dear Mrs. Haizlip,

I am currently a senior (graduating in exactly seventeen days!) at Goucher College. I am a psychology major and sociology minor. I have spent the last year working on a senior thesis about students' ways of thinking and talking about Affirmative Action and racial diversity.

A few months ago, while I was home for Christmas break, my mother called me into her bedroom. She was watching a talk show, I believe it was *Oprah* and you were one of the guests. . . . I have just recently finished *The Sweeter the Juice* and have not been able to stop talking about it ever since. I plan to give a copy to each of the members of my thesis committee.

I have become really interested in identity and the rules we use to form our identities as black, white, female, male, heterosexual, homosexual, etc. And have wondered about the power necessary to make and break those rules.

I remember early in the book, when you discuss the annual census. One year you would find your "black" relative in the books, and the next year, that same relative would all of a sudden be "white." How did their lives change as a result of the totally subjective perspective of the (white, male) census taker? How is the "invisible" secret that light skinned blacks carried around with them (abandoning their black roots and gaining more access and privilege within a white world), different from the "secret" that gays and lesbians must keep to protect themselves, choosing carefully which parts of themselves to reveal? It seems as if we all balance precariously between visibility and invisibility depending on context and circumstance.

Upon finishing your book, I immediately wanted to share my thesis with you. I consider this paper a work in progress and plan to continue my research this summer and next year in Boston, working on anti-racism training and education within schools. Thank you for sharing your story. The hundreds of new questions I have reflect how much I have learned from you.

Sincerely,

Angela DiMaria, Maryland

Dear Ms. Haizlip,

Just wanted to let you know how much I enjoyed hearing you speak at Elliott Bay Books, the other evening. What an amazing and fascinating story! I can't wait to read "the rest of the story" in your book.

I'm now inspired to pick up my family's genealogy work that I've let collect dust in my closet for a year. I wonder if the Dutch/German/French heritage I already know about may also have "roots in other gardens," possibly some African American roots. I know that there are some black Dotson (my last name) families around, but don't know how that came about. I think some of my shirttail relatives owned slaves, possibly in Kentucky. Maybe they took on my family's name? Or did some of my relatives marry or have relations with the slaves? Lots of question marks.

Also, my grandfather once told a story about his mother's dad who supposedly was lynched for defending a black man, maybe some time around the 1870s. I'd love to find out if that was really fact or fiction. So many different paths to explore.

Your story certainly raises some complicated but interesting questions. What does it mean to be a "white" American or a "black" American or of "mixed" race? And do these arbitrary labels even matter? Or even if they do matter, should they?

Anyways, your story really got my family history juices flowing again! I hope your book will inspire others to explore theirs. I wish you much success . . . in rediscovering and reuniting your family.

Pam Dotson, Washington

Dear Shirlee,

As I sit in 30th Street station in Philadelphia, I finished *The Sweeter the Juice*! Thank you. As a Wellesley classmate from the other side of campus and in so many ways from another world — WASP Cleveland — I missed so much but I didn't know it. Your courage and your search have raised questions for me for sure and in truth it should for all of us. My life continues to be separate and I know I haven't made possibilities for it to be different even though if it were presented to me I would welcome it.

In my work with independent schools I try to help schools work on their climate, their curriculum and their inclusion. I would love to have you address an audience from our schools (85 in all). . . . I for one don't want to give up hope that this country can tear down the walls! I am sharing the book with all I meet and am thankful the Post gave you coverage or I might have missed it. I'm sure you are being overwhelmed with responses but I'll hope to hear from you.

All best wishes,
Sarah MacCracken Donnelly [Wellesley] '59,
Maryland

(Author's note: I responded to my friend Sarah's note and later addressed a large group of her professional colleagues.)

Dear Ms. Haizlip

I enjoyed reading your book very much. I am now sending it as a present to my father. But before I did I had to go back and see if your mother and her sister ever discussed the fact that they were living in different races. And I found that in your book they did not, though perhaps they have since then.

I am trained as both a biologist and an anthropologist, but still it was many years after I completed my training that I finally asked myself, Why is it that a person who is any part black, colored, African American, etc. is considered to belong to that group while the reverse is not true? When Americans think that way they are denying everyday commonsense biology and affirming the pseudo biology of race. Since a race has to be a closed group, Americans have agreed to deny what they know and accept the mass delusion that they "know" who all the White people are and who all the Black people are.

When I came upon some information that I thought might help break down this delusion I decided to write about it and get it published. I wrote two versions, one that says brothers and one that says sisters. The brothers' version has been published in the *Houston Peace News* and in the *Dialogue Racism Newsletter.* Though my phone number was printed, no one has called me. This version was written for the Houston NOW newsletter, which went defunct before they could print it. Nevertheless part of my purpose was served because some people saw it and thought about it.

I hope lots of people are buying your book and thinking about the issues it raises. I believe that the time for this issue has come. In the case of my discovery (already well known to African Americans here about), it relates as much to male domination as it does to race. . . . If you know of any other places I could get this published, or other people who would like to do research write a longer article or a book on the same topic, please write me.

I thank you for your contribution to the same cause.

Nancy Edwards, Texas

THE PERSONAL IS POLITICAL IN RACISM TOO

by Nancy Edwards

As we all know, "All women are sisters," but Americans have difficulty extending this relationship to our sisters in other races. In part this is true because we believe that other races are only our very distant cousins. In east Texas, however, this relationship can be much closer. Not so long ago in this part of the country it was possible for a White man to have two wives, one White and one Black. Provided that he was only legally married to the White wife, he was free to treat his Black family any way he chose. He could keep them hidden or he could house them next door to his White family and neither the law nor society could stop him. And when he died he could cut off his Black children if he chose, or will them half his estate.

This practice continued close enough to the present day that many of these half siblings are still living. And though we have heard from some Black people who believe that their foremothers were exploited by White men, we have yet to hear the reactions of these older White people who have Black half siblings.

I believe that it would contribute to the improvement of race relations in the United States if some of the White descendants of these families were to acknowledge their Black siblings, in private at first and then perhaps in public. This would help to contradict the myth that races are distinct human groups, which can not be united into a single family.

I am interested in pursuing this issue further. If any reader is interested in collaborating on this project, please call me. . . .

Dear Shirlee,

I work in the renewal parts office of General Electric Company in Salem, Va. One day I had to leave a little early and when I got home Oprah Winfrey was on. I heard the woman talking as I went downstairs to the den, before I saw the picture I knew it had to be you, from what you said.

You cannot even begin to realize how much it meant to me to see that show. That beautiful mother of yours, such a lady. I loved every minute of it and wish it could have been longer and you tell us more. I loved all the relatives that were interviewed and their attitudes of not being ashamed of their background. I did not get the name of the young man on the stage but I love him for the way he feels.

I am going to read the book again. I feel I may have missed something and I can tell you that much of what you told I remembered from the book.

When your husband mentioned Kernersville, N.C., I laughed. I have relatives there. . . . They used to live on Coltrane Street. Their reason for moving, you guessed it. The neighborhood was being taken over by black people.

I hope you continue to research and do a sequel to your

book. I still do not understand why your mother was left behind. That's why I have to reread the book. . . .

Sincerely,

Joan K. Shannon, Virginia

Dear Mrs. Haizlip:

I recently finished reading your book, *The Sweeter the Juice,* and wanted to tell you how much I enjoyed it. I found your words intriguing, saddening and was touched by your feelings and emotions about your family.

I think it is a tragic society we live in where we spend so much time pointing out the differences between ourselves, instead of trying to find the similarities that bind us together as human being. I looked at the photo of Grace Morris, circa 1921, and showed it to my father. He casually mentioned that she could easily have fit into a picture of my grandmother and her eight sisters (white Virginians). The familiar similarities are within us all. Many things that are wrong with this world could be changed if we only looked at ourselves as a part of everyone else around us.

I thank you for sharing your experiences with me, as a reader. You've helped me understand better the anger and bitterness some of my friends carry around with them. I hope that my two-year-old daughter can grow to live in a society that is not prejudiced toward shades of color, but appreciative for the beauty that lies within the multitude of hues.

Sincerely,

Maxine E. Walker, Texas

Dear Shirley,

I bought *TSTJ* yesterday and finished it today. I resented every interruption of my reading it and when I finished I wished it hadn't been over so quickly. Each character was so real. Most of all, there was a lot to mull when the story ended.

I laughed and cried, especially for Margaret, your mother. And fond memories of my grandfather were brought back with our recollections of your father and grandfather. My grandfather was a minister, too. He was also underpaid and sometimes not paid. But there was always food on the table because he had a vegetable garden in the backyard. I don't recall if it was your father or grandfather who said something about "plenty" at the end of a meal, but Grandpa used to say something like that. I wonder if it's a universal term that ministers use. Maybe it's from the Bible. I still have handwritten sermons of Grandpa's.

I could see myself in your description of Wellesley years. I think we all have our levels of discomfort when we change schools. Mine was at Westlake School for Girls. Many of the students had been in the school since kindergarten and I felt uncomfortable that they were years ahead of me in refined manners by the time I started in the tenth grade. By the way, Shirley Temple was there at the time.

I was so touched by your telling about meeting relatives for the first time. Same uneasy feelings came over Bruce and me when we visited relatives who hadn't known we existed until we showed up at their doorsteps. You have so much in common and so little in common and the only way out of the awkward situation is to look at old photographs and talk about their pets. I wonder if we'll ever get around to talking about politics or current events. Just too tenuous a relationship to risk it.

Shirlee, it was truly an American story and so intimately told that I feel as if I know you. Fascinating watching the you that you are today evolve. Can't wait for your next book. No matter what subject matter you choose, it will be a good read, I'm sure.

        Fondly,
        Marilyn Moe, California

Dear Shirlee Taylor Haizlip,

    Since I read your book, I have been thinking of you. I'd hoped to invite you and your mother to lunch to discuss the book (your life and thoughts!) with you, but I couldn't find you in the phone book either here on St. John or in Los Angeles.

    I couldn't attend your reading at the bookshop (at the Purple Door in Cruz Bay) because we flew straight through from St. Thomas to Honolulu for my husband to be a candidate for the ministry of the First Unitarian Church of Honolulu. He got the job and we've returned here for two more weeks for him to write.

    While we were in Honolulu, an African American woman in the church noticed I was just finishing your book. . . . My friend is asking her family to read the book so that when she goes home this summer, she and her family can discuss race issues in a more objective way than immediately bringing up her own pain. She and I had a good discussion. . . .

    I liked the way you wrote about situations in such a non-judgmental way. The conclusions were obvious. Particularly vivid was the contrast between your mother's life and her sister's. The African American side had achieved and experienced such a rich life. Do you think that their (your) authenticity gave you all a strong basis while the white side always felt the insecurity of possible exposure?

    Also you had the strong support of a caring community. Besides racial identity, the church community gives that. Our family has certainly felt that, both pluses and minuses. The importance of caring role models offering strong expectations certainly shows in our book. . . .

In 1967 we had a black foster son. It worked pretty well because we lived in E. Palo Alto, a mixed community. He loved to push people's buttons. One time in DuPars, a coffee shop in Encino, he called all the way across the dining room, "Hi, Grampa," to my very blond dad. Heads turned. At first, Daddy's mouth fell open; then he caught Greg's humor, and they laughed and laughed. I've always wondered how much prejudice Greg had to face. He's had a hard life.

When we lived in E. Palo Alto was when we had our first black friends. (I never know the right words to use.) My friend had a secretive pride that her daughters were light, and indeed her school age daughter was very popular. She loved her darker children just as much, but seemed to have lower expectations of them.

As a schoolteacher I felt I had high expectations for all my kids, but it often took a long time for me to gain the children's trust, and I could almost hear them wondering, "Who is she that she can tell me I can be a lawyer?"—or whatever. Of course the scariest part is the project kids with no decent examples, the young mothers so beaten down. In Tampa the Urban League and other groups are recognizing the chasm. It seems that only the achievers and those acting out get attention. The problems of poverty and poor parenting. And so many poor people, black and white.

Yet I feel we are coming along. To me the sixties are just yesterday. To me the hardest part is making conversation. Being of different races is like fear of land mines. I never know if something I praise, like music and showing joy, will be taken

as condescension. I have been privileged, but I've also worked
hard, taken chances and been persistent. I hope that our grandchildren will work to conserve our works. I hope your mother's
sadness is alleviated.

Sincerely yours,
Nancy S. Young, Hawaii

Dear Shirlee,

After watching you and your family on Oprah's show, I
couldn't wait to read your book. I immediately put a "hold" on
it at the Library through my modem (fantastic technology). I
finished it yesterday; it is fascinating, to say the least.

My son and I did research on our genealogy at the National
Archives in D.C. in April of 1991. As I read your book, I could
picture you scanning the microfilm the same as we did. We
have no history such as you were able to gather, but I had
urged and prodded and begged until there was quite a store of
"childhood memories" to include in our book. As the editor, I
had to chop some a bit; and with others, I called for just a teeny
bit more.

I congratulate you on a wonderful story. I've written to a
friend in Columbus, Ohio, who also has a mixed background to
recommend that she read it.

I happen to be a child of mid-European ancestors. I never
knew a black person until I worked for the government.
There, I selected a few as friends. I chose just as carefully as
with the white friends, looking for some common interest. My
Columbus friend and I used to go to the opera together, took
our children to see the *Nutcracker*, and crocheted our afghans
during lunch breaks at work. My daughter and I spent a
weekend at her house, and if she ever gets to my neighbor-

hood, she says she'll stay with me. This promise is on going for about five years now, but something always comes up. Her name is Shirlee, too.

           Sincerely,

           Dorothy Byrne, Kentucky

P.S. I've used Dixie Peach for about a year, because my hair has lost its youthful sheen. I had no idea it was Negro-inspired.

Dear Mrs. Haizlip,

    Less than an hour ago I finished reading your family history, *The Sweeter the Juice.* I found the experience of reading about your discovery of your family to be transfixing.

    I believe I saw you and one of your relatives on the Oprah Winfrey show some time ago. After the program aired, the idea of being part of a multi-racial family and the notion of "six degrees of separation" captivated me and my friends. We spent many hours trying to come to terms with our notions of race and racism. I regretted not having made note of the name of the author of the book that was presented on the Oprah Winfrey show that day.

    When I came across *The Sweeter the Juice,* I was thrilled to have found the book that had proven inspirational even before I had bought and read it. My goal in writing to you was to thank you for the time and effort you put into telling your family's story to me and many others.

    I believe that writing this book must have been an act of courage. I felt as if you let me see layers of truth that could have been easily removed from these pages, in an acquiescence to what you called politesse of deceit. You could have sheltered your family and readers from certain aspects of your history without having damaged your story. Thank you for unveiling these extra layers of truth. By sharing some of the sadder elements of your family history, such as the impact of William Morris Sr.'s alcoholism, Julian Jr.'s troubles and Percy Taylor's lonely death, you provided an excellent measure of the successes your parents and you and your husband have experienced. By failing to tidy-up and resolve your own feelings about white people and your multiracial family, and admitting to your own ambiguousness, you allowed the rest of us to admit and explore our own feelings. Few works of history can accomplish so lofty a goal.

As I settle *The Sweeter the Juice* into position on my bookshelf, I know it is a book I will reread. And a book from which I will take ideas that will help me construct the rest of my life. Thank you again.

I hope this letter arrives finding you and the members of your family well. You painted such an intimate portrait of them that I feel I could ask about each by name, as if we were having coffee and I was asking about the relatives of a friend. Maybe someday there will be a sequel for those of us left wondering what happened next.

Sincerely,

Donna Cooper, Utah

Dear Ms. Haizlip:

I rushed out and bought your book after reading *The Washington Post*'s spread in Style, for the subject of passing is one that I have felt for some time needs to be brought out of the closet and discussed seriously by all Americans, most particularly those who cannot bring themselves to believe that there is at least one black berry on almost every white American tree.

Yours is a fascinating, tragic story and well told. I found it totally engrossing. . . . With all good wishes for your continued success and the hope that your story may lead the way to elimination of the ridiculous and cruel "one-drop rule" from our national consciousness.

> Sincerely,
> E. Pratt Cheely, Washington, D.C.

Dear Ms. Haizlip:

I have just finished reading your book *The Sweeter the Juice* and wanted to tell you how much I enjoyed it and to thank you for sharing the history of your family. Not only was it well written and a good genealogical study, but it had several aspects that I identified with personally and I feel that I am probably somehow distantly related to you.

Three of my four grandparents were of Irish ancestry. My mother's grandparents were from County Tipperary as was your great grandmother. My mother's maiden name was Everett and her father's family had been in the country since colonial days and were part of the Morris family. My mother says that the name Morris was derived from "Moorish," which would suggest racial intermixture even before arrival to the New World. Besides the Morrises and the Everetts, we have a lot of Margarets (I'm one) as you do. (Also my father's name is Harold as is your husband's.)

My family has lived in New Haven for years and I grew up on Townsend Avenue in the Annex across the harbor. If you continue down Townsend Avenue, of course, you reach Morris Cove and near the end of Townsend Ave., just before Lighthouse Beach, is the Morris House. Before it became a museum, descendants of the Morrises lived in the house and my grandparents lived there briefly after their marriage (1915). . . .

Your description of life in New Haven and its environs was

of much interest. Like your daughters, I attended Wilbur Cross High School and graduated in 1963 (I wonder if Cross still holds its graduation ceremonies in Woolsey Hall). I then graduated from Southern Connecticut State College in '67 and while a student there, I dated a Yale graduate student from Malawi in Central Africa (Yale undergrads, still all male at the time, didn't date Southern Ct. girls, but I guess the foreign students didn't know the difference). He opened my eyes to an area of study not covered at that time in the schools—Africa. (World History was, of course, basically European history.) This was very exciting and I went on to teach for two years in Ethiopia with the Peace Corps and then to obtain a Master's degree in African Studies at UCLA. More recently, I have taken an African-American History class at West L.A. College and gained a different perspective on the history of the U.S. I would be very proud to have African blood in my lineage and after reading your book, I now know that I probably do since part of the family at least has lived in this country since colonial days. Another common denominator we have is that from Connecticut, we've both ended up in the L.A. area (also we both have two daughters). I love the multi-ethnicity of the city and although disheartened by its many problems, I still have great hopes for its future and the future of our children. Thank you again.

                    Sincerely,
                    Peggy Preston Kharraz, California

Dear Shirlee,

    Allow me to say on the first line of this letter that I am a seventy-eight-year-old white woman who has lived in Kentucky all my life.

I caught your name and the fact you had written a book from the Oprah Winfrey show. I noted that your name was Haizlip and at sometime your people had lived in North Carolina. As the enclosed chart shows my husband's great grandmother was born a Haizlip and married a Morris from North Carolina. The Haizlip family was also from N.C.

I have been active in genealogy in the past and have compiled five books that now repose in the Library of Congress.

I was completely fascinated with your book and read it from "Kiver to Kiver" in two days.

You seemed to have a more affluent and intellectual background than I ever enjoyed. Our parents were interested in our education. I am a child of the great Depression so I attended College whenever possible, coming home and going back when a bit more money was forthcoming.

After my children left home for out of state colleges I again attended college but never did get my degree. My husband got his Bachelors ten years after entering college. He would teach and then go to school and finally made it. He is to this day a scholar so he had no problem passing the courses offered to him. He was from a family of eight children so many times he helped the younger children from his meager salary. Once he taught only six months and the salary was $50 per month.

I worked in a factory and we lived apart the first year of our marriage while he finished school. That following fall he obtained a school about fifty miles from where I worked so again we lived apart through the week.

I relate some of the above to make you realize there are ambitious white people who have financial problems. Presently I live in a nice six-room brick house in a good neighborhood. I have two sons and five grandchildren who are all doing well. My oldest son is a graduate of Georgia Tech and has his master's at the University of Houston and is doing quite well as a chemical engineer in the oil industry in Houston. My younger son graduated from Yale '65 Davenport College, graduated from Vanderbilt '69 Medical School, and has his private practice in Nashville. His oldest daughter graduated from Harvard, got her master's in England and is now in second year at Harvard Law School. The grandsons are still in high school.

After WW2 I went back to work at GE and for thirty years was employed there making possible our ability to send our sons to school and to take nice vacations. I am a Christian and a Methodist and do believe all of the above was given to me by a Gracious God so I do not mean to boast. I am thankful for all the blessings I have enjoyed.

It seems this is a day when people proclaim they are not a bigot or worse still, a racist. I really don't know if I am either or not. I grew up in a rural community and saw very few black people until I was grown. When my children were away in College I attended a small local College and had my first Black classmates. I enjoyed being in class with them and felt close enough to one young woman to ask this question. What is it that Whites do that "bugs" you most? She told me quite frankly for us to always ask a Black if they knew every black in town like they knew no whites. I was guilty as charged but have never done it again. I might add we are still friends as she works in AV section of the library and I see her often.

I am in a monthly reading club and I influenced a Black woman to join the group. She rides the bus to the meetings and I take her home, as the bus does not run late by her home. The first home we ever owned was in a white neighborhood with one black family straight across from us. We never experienced any discomfort from this arrangement.

Now here is something I do not understand about Black people. There is not a person living in America who ever owned a black slave so why harp on the situation? It was horrible, unthinkable, and anything else that describes the situation but how is this generation responsible? Some of my ancestors came down from Maryland and brought slaves with them and kept them until the Civil War. This family name was Acton.

I have a Black friend in northern Indiana who carries this name. She has visited in my home; we went ancestor hunting a few miles out of town together. She had a real piece of luck. The white lady had a powder horn with the slave's name on it and presented it to the ancestor.

If there is one thing that makes my blood boil it's the existence of intimidation. I think that is the worst thing between the races in my lifetime. Being afraid to speak out on opinions, and of course not getting justice in the courts. Thank goodness Kentucky is not far enough South to be excessive in "White man's justice." My grandfather was in the Civil War on the Northern side.

Now here is a question I sincerely do not know the answer to. What do Black people want of Whites? Blacks have their beauty contests that I don't suppose we are welcome to compete in, they have their Black Parades and other events that I suppose are exclusive events.

Here is one thing that I think Ky did to their dying shame. I was told that when the then Cassius Clay won medals in boxing and came back to his native Louisville for recognition he was just still a little colored boy and in his disgust threw his medals in the River. I wish this were not true. No one can clean up an act such as this.

All Haizlips in Ky settled in Edmonson County near Mammoth Cave. They have dark hair and eyes and maybe mixed blood. I am Scotch-Irish, fair blue eyed.

> Bye now,
> Eula Mitchell, Kentucky

Dear Ms. Haizlip,

I talked with you on January 29. I told you a story about contacting a person (Barbara Gash) on e-mail, letting her know that we might be related. Barbara and I talked on the phone and discovered we had family from the same area—Buncombe County, North Carolina. But, Barbara said she didn't think we were related. I asked why she thought we weren't related. She said we couldn't be related because she was black. I said that that didn't absolutely mean we weren't related. She said her Father was going to a family reunion in South Carolina. I asked her if I could send her some family pedigree charts on my GASH line.

My g-g-grandmother's name was Selina Gash. Barbara called me back several days later. She was very surprised to see the name Selina Gash as she had an aunt named Selina Gash. But, Barbara doesn't seem to want to pursue the connection any further—at least for now.

Now a little bit about me. I'm fifty-three, work as a civilian employee here at McClellan Air Force Base near Sacramento. I am the base focal point for computer security. A job I plan to relinquish in another year and one half, when I retire. At times I'm not real clear on what being married means, but my life partner, Clark, and I consider ourselves married, for just over twelve years. My time in retirement won't involve the day to day work, as I've been doing, but many other things that I haven't had the time to do. Like writing a book about my Uncle Emil "Scotty" Scott who was in China from 1938 until his death as pilot of a DC-2 in March of 1942. I'd also like to write a book about his widow, my aunt, who was interned by the Japanese, when Manila fell. She lives in San Francisco. Clark and I own a place on the beach on Kauai and spend a couple of weeks there each year. Just got back last month. Flyer included with this package. 10% off if you're ever interested. When I retire we'd both like to get out of Sacramento to an area not so crowded and with cleaner air.

The family reunion I mentioned in my recent post card to you was great. This reunion generates itself around my brother's five children who are now grown and have their own kids. About 25 folks this past year. I will be attending another family reunion on my mother's side of the family in Dallas over the Labor Day Weekend. My mother's side has the Gash line. I've mentioned my slight beginnings on color research to my nieces and nephews. All they've said so far is "Oh?" Just a quizzical, "Oh"—nothing else.

I really did like and relate to your book. I kept tearing Post-its into small pieces to mark the pages I wanted to ask you about. Now that I've read your book I will be looking at my genealogy research in a slightly different light. Especially when I read a census report listing Gash family members and slaves in the same household or farm/plantation.

Well this has been some letter. I hope you didn't mind me writing to you and writing to you and writing to you and writing to you—"yeah, yeah, Tom I get the picture." Also please keep the enclosed photo.

Take care and let me hear from you when you have the time.

Sincerely,
Tom O. Moore, Jr., California

P.S. If you couldn't tell, I loved your book.

Poetic License

I am the family face,
Flesh perishes, I live on,
Projecting trait and trace
Through time to times anon,
And leaping from place to place
Over oblivion.

— *Thomas Hardy, "Heredity"*

Something in the story of *The Sweeter the Juice* connected with dozens of people who write poetry—some seriously, some as an avocation. Included here are a few poems that came with the letters.

Waltz: A Preacher Teaches His Daughter to Dance

Autumn in Ansonia,
Connecticut: the deep places
still frosted in hard dew on a late afternoon
when the sun finally reaches them,
at a slant.
The river, the town, the factories of
my father's parishioners
industrial and rural/white for the rest and black for us,
the same smokestacks and brick,
one set of miniature cliffs behind, wall
of pine and October brilliance.
But tonight
The high school dance, velvet toes touch
the last frozen drops on still pliant grass
and wing-tips tied tight spring up
for a cavalcade of the modern dances
—Charleston, Black Bottom
Wing, Be-Bop—
then the timeless:
the waltz.
My father
slender/sophisticated/stern, that afternoon before,
rehearsed me,
bowed and anchored me, in leading arms, just as he
was taking the town on a stately free turn
of truth for forty years,
preaching the partnership of black to black
in small white New England,
the grace of our race:
The grace,
and he taught it to me

while he pushed the music outward
as local politics swirled into local pastoring
and widening to the state's Jewish governor.
who swung around to pull in the nation's Irish Catholic
    president,
both urgent for support and its noble partner, just
    wisdom—
but he knew my father knew
that waltz is to life
like autumn is to coming winter:
the variety of color in beautied storm,
torn and tumbling down cliff to river, on,
and that is how he took me into the step—
he moved, oak brown, I flew, birch light, two leaves
"being blown in patterns around the dance floor."

  —Emily Holcombe for Shirlee Taylor Haizlip
   (quotation and story are hers)

I Am Me

My great grandmother was colored
  My grandmother was Negro
   My Mommy was Black
 And, Now I am an African American
Why are my People trying to find out what they are
 They tell me we were kings and queens in Africa
  Does that make us African?
My great grandmother says her mother was half white
 My grandmother says at birth she was real light
  My Mommy has long black Indian hair

I was born a light brownish red, and now I am a Cocoa
      Cola brown
            What are my people?
      Are we white with an Indian flair?
      Are we brown with straight hair?
            My great grandmother says
      My great grandfather's people were Indian
            My grandmother says
      My Grandfather's father was an Indian too
My Mommy says, my Daddy was a deep chocolate man
            I look in the mirror
                  What do I see?
A Member of the human race with a very special face.

      —*Susan Talbert*

Gifts in the face of prejudice

      She chose song
      to bring purpose
      Me, I write.
      She, chose Jazz.
      Poetry, my choice.
      We are sisters.
      Born unto the spirits
            of mother earth.
      Mentored by mothers of color
            from the past.
      Our colors abound.
      Most brilliant in the fall.
      Radiant by our glistening
            rivers of red.

Flourishing among
 nations of man.
Our talents to be critiqued
  but,
like the spectacular rainbow,
our colors are meant to be seen
 beyond black or white.
Appreciated for the variety
and beauty within.

  —Janice Chapin, Missouri

They Say I'm Black
dedicated to Shirlee Taylor Haizlip

They say I'm black
They say I'm dark
They say I'm light
They even say I'm bright,
but would you think I may be white?
They say I can sing
They say I can shout
They say you can find me inside the church or even out
They say I'm black.
They say I can play ball
They say I spend all my money at the mall
They say that I am of beautiful queens with royal blood
 in me
that can be seen
They say I am black.
They say that I was the first mother of earth
Oh yes, I was the one to give you birth

They say I'm black.
They say that I was enslaved for hundreds of years,
It was my ancestors bravery that brought them through the
toils and the tears
They say I'm black.
    Bronzed my people in gold
    Lashed at them for growing old
    Accused them of wrongful doing
    Cursed them to the highest
    Killed them for no reason at all.
They still say that I too, am BLACK!

—Katouri Wilson, North Carolina

17

The Last Word

A PASSING STORY

"A light-skinned black man who pretended to be white so he could fight for the U.S. military in World War II was honored posthumously Monday for outstanding bravery.

"Calvin Clark Davis flew fifty missions in the Pacific theater—enough to exempt him from further combat—but he then volunteered to fight in Europe, where he was killed during a bombing run over Germany." For his efforts. Davis, the descendant of a black slave and a white plantation owner, received the World War II Victory Medal and the Purple Heart.

"Davis was one of many blacks who passed themselves off as white so they wouldn't be relegated to noncombat duty under segregation rules. . . . Orphaned as a child, Davis was raised in poverty by his older sister. . . .'" Lester

Reed, 88, a former classmate in the rural northeastern Michigan village where they had gone to school, said, "'He looked as white as you or me. His sister was black, but nobody paid any attention to it.' Representative John Conyers summed it all up by saying, 'He should be honored not only for his heroic efforts as a soldier, but for his willingness to serve a country that did not necessarily want his service.'"

(From "WWII Hero Faked Being White, Gets Honors,"
Los Angeles Times, *February 19, 2002)*

Two of my uncles, Sumner Morris and Eddie Morris, served in the First World War as white soldiers. I have pictures of both of them in their uniforms. Eddie was a victim of the great influenza epidemic of 1918 and died while he was in the service. He was just eighteen.

My mother welcomed the millennium with Harold and me at a fast-moving party at the Ebell Club, a women's club in Los Angeles. Also at our invitation, our octogenarian, former-actress friend, Helen Andrews, had a ruffled red chiffon evening gown from her glory days in the forties dry-cleaned so that she could join us. Helen had been our neighbor and friend for ten years. In the last five years she had become an extended family member for whom we made dinner every day. During that time, she and Mother had become close.

Pattee flew in from Connecticut with a friend, and Melissa took off from a show to help us bid in this once-in-a-lifetime New Year.

Amid cascades of hundreds of purple and silver balloons and centerpieces of fragrant star lilies, the old ones glowed with attention and wonder. We moved from Caribbean rhythms in the dining room to swing and jazz in the salon, to the intimacy of a piano bar in the library. Mother and Helen didn't miss a beat. My mother was eighty-eight and Helen was eighty-nine. Neither one had thought she would be alive to usher in a new century and a new millennium.

During her last visit to California, I often talked with my mother about what it meant to find Grace and the rest of her family, both living and dead. Sometimes we talked in the garden, in the afternoon sun. Other times, the guest room with my grandfather's comfortable rocking chair enveloping my mother's small frame was the setting for our reveries.

It was agonizing for me to tell her that our friend Helen, who had become her special Los Angeles companion, had died. Helen was one of her anchors of comfort in Los Angeles. She had asked me to give Mother one of her porcelain dogs from a cherished collection. The dog guarded Mother's bed table at night.

Each time we walked by the garden window that had been Helen's, Mother sighed. When we sat on the garden bench near the white rosebush that had been planted to memorialize Helen's dog, Pamela, Mother spoke of their happy girlish times together. With each other, they had become young again. With unquestioned authenticity, they could run on about Model Ts, flapper dresses, Prohibition, the New Deal, World Wars I and II, rations, and the like.

Of all the things that had happened to my mother as she lived through the hours of her eighty-plus years, she said, the most significant was finding Grace.

There was no way that any conversation about her family could center on the present. She always slipped back to the past, when she was that orphaned four-year-old leading her two-year-old, crippled brother by his hand. She was glad to know, she said, that her father's alcoholism was the source of most of the family's trauma. She wavered back and forth as to whether she felt sorry for him. Some days she did; others she didn't. She developed a new sympathy for her older brother Bill, because she admired the fact that he had taken on the job of caring for her siblings. She understood what an undertaking it had to be for him to shepherd around her sister and her brothers during the country's hard economic times. And then to have the racial identity issue always hovering about.

But still, there was that nagging pull, that little voice that said, "Yes, but he could have contacted me." Then she remembers that Bill's daughters, her nieces, have claimed her, and she is glad.

I ask her if she still has anger, grief, and regret. She speaks of anger over the wasted years, anger over prejudice and discrimination, anger that it took so long to find her family. She still grieves for the mother she never knew and the sister who was lost to her for seventy-six years. She regrets that her father and brothers died without knowing her and me and my sisters and brother.

Nonetheless, her overriding feeling is happiness that the mystery of her missing family has been solved. Joy that she met and knew her sister. Wonder that her grand-nieces and -nephews send her notes and cards and are curious about her life.

"Hollywood sure has some *good*-looking firemen," Mother said as two firemen, one holding her hand and talking quietly to her, carried her on a chair down the stairs and out to a waiting emergency ambulance. This after she, with flushed cheeks, clutched at her chest and spat out that she couldn't breathe. A visiting daughter, Deirdre, calmly became the brigadier general as she issued orders that would save my mother's life. For the first time in my life I called 911, and the operator, hooked up to the city's vast emergency apparatus, guided our steps for the next few critical minutes.

The "good-looking firemen" supplied oxygen and leading-men smiles, which revived my mother enough that she knew she was probably out of danger. At the hospital, the diagnosis was variable: some said asthma, others said emphysema. All agreed that it was a serious and debilitating lung disease that would not get better. Their contemporary medical catchphrase for it was COPD: chronic obstructive pulmonary disease. There was no way I could not wonder whether my mother was a victim of the secondhand smoke that she had breathed all those years living with my cigarette-smoking father and others.

As we waited for Mother to be assigned to a bed for a four-day hospital stay, she looked down at her hand. "It's time for you to have this," she said, pointing to her favorite ring. It was the ring that my father had made for her, after I had given her a pair of antique diamond earrings from my godmother, Rosa. Rosa had made the gift to me on my sixteenth birthday, but I'd had no interest in antique drop earrings at that time. "You know this ring will come back to you at the right time," she had always said.

I thought then that Mother was trying to tell me something before she headed home to Connecticut. I was not yet ready to receive my gift. She insisted, though, because she knew she would probably be hospitalized again and she did not want to lose our cherished family antique in the process. Reluctantly, I put the ring on. I have not removed it since.

Now my mother spends her time resting in either a bed or a chair. She lives in a nursing home fifteen minutes away from Pattee's house. Most days, Pattee or one of her sons visits and makes sure Mother is well cared for. Her bones are frail and she is unsteady on her feet. Sometimes it is difficult for her to breathe. She is tethered to an oxygen-producing valve. Her mind is mostly clear. Her sense of humor is still there. And when her head is cocked at a particular angle in a particular light, when she has on her lipstick and earrings, there are strong vestiges of her former beauty.

I ask her what she is thinking about. "A lot of things," she replies. I mull that over for a while. Indians. Africans. Scots. Irish. Italian. English. Mulattoes. Slaves. A motherless child, paternal abandonment, separation from her siblings, foster mothers, life on a farm, an eccentric guardian, segregation, an early marriage, a move from South to North, from big city to small town, integration, four children, two stepdaughters, churches to preside over, visiting ministers, cross-country travels, politics and politicians, civil rights, women's rights, cotillions, college educations, weddings, grandchildren, widowhood, old age, infirmities. Life. All enveloped in the mystery of race and the ravages of racism. All abated by a large and loving biological family that she produced and an even larger family of her heart. A lot of things.

I marvel at my mother's equanimity. Were she not encumbered by health problems, she said, she would be "looking for another man." At ninety.

I guess I could not hope for better than that.

Epilogue

On the morning of December 11, 2002, my sister Pattee called to tell me that my mother's doctor advised that she should be moved to the hospice in Branford, Connecticut. I knew immediately that meant my mother's death was imminent. Two days later I was on a plane east. During the flight, my emotions shut down. I was all cerebellum. I began to think about how her life should be reflected in her obituary; I began to make plans for her funeral.

In the center of a quiet, tree-lined cove known as Lamphiers Lane, Connecticut Hospice hugs the end of a long, sloping drive that curves around the edge of the Connecticut shoreline. Built in a modified U, the building's wings become outstretched arms that beckon and welcome. Glass vistas on all three floors frame the sparkling Long Island Sound. Boats large and small are visible through the floor-to-ceiling windows. Patients' beds are all angled to the sea and the light. Working fireplaces dot the corridors. It is a beautiful, gracious, and graceful facility.

Outside, manicured lawns drop off at the shoreline. A gazebo houses a small, perfectly formed Christmas tree, covered in white lights. A dozen yards offshore sits Lovers' Island, a small mustache-shaped piece of land, with one side of the mustache bushier than the other. One can keep track of the tides by watching how much of the island's tiny beaches are submerged. At low tide, you can walk across the sand to the island.

The place was decorated tastefully for Christmas. Candles, poinsettias, and greens prevailed. Every day, a band of variegated volunteers brought pets, children, carols, crafts, spiritual balm, and Christmas gifts for the dying. In ways it was like a school getting ready for the holidays. But none of the students would be returning to school after the season of light was over.

At first, Mother was put into the pediatric ward because of a scarcity of beds. She was its only occupant. A beaming sun and a drowsy moon wearing a purple sleeping cap were her painted companions. If she looked at the ceiling, she could see kites, balloons, stars, airplanes, rockets, and rainbows. For my mother, who loved animals, the decor was a feast. Should she choose to cast her eyes downward at the floor, she could focus on choo-choo trains and a whimsical menagerie of giraffes, teddy bears, crocodiles, elephants, chickens, curly-haired sheep, and the other icons of happy childhoods. It was not lost on me that she had had no such room like this when she was a child. How wonderful, I thought, that she could experience it now.

Although there is a variety of brochures and how-tos in the literature made available to the family of hospice patients, it is hard to know what to do in a place that has dying at its center. I spent most of my time at my mother's bedside, talking with her, singing her favorite hymns and gospel tunes, rubbing her forehead, her arm, her shoulder, holding her hand. When she was sleeping, I tried halfheartedly to read.

Outside at water's edge, a flock of sociable Canadian geese was making a stopover. Patients and visitors alike followed their daily gambols. Sometimes as many as thirty-eight geese stood at attention on the lawn, all peering in the same direction, waiting for a signal that only they could hear. Floating in the water between the island and the shore, a flock of ducks competed for territory with a pair of swans. Brown squirrels with generous tails, sparrows, doves, and Mother's favorites, scarlet cardinals, busied themselves outside the windows. Sometimes, patients' family members strolled the lawns. Throbbing life was everywhere outside. Ebbing life was everywhere inside.

At night I would go "home" to a cozy Victorian house built in 1864 near the Long Island Sound in New Haven. My hostess was an old friend I had known since my WNET days in New York. She left me and Harold to take care of the house and her cats while she spent Christmas in Virginia. It was comforting to be around old things that had history and their own stories to tell. I thought about the many previous occupants of that house who had died and the circumstances of their deaths.

After several days, my mother was moved to an adult room, facing the water. Word had gotten around among the staff that she was a "celebrity." There was a great deal of curiosity about the rainbow-colored tribe that traipsed in to see the lady whose race they could not quite pin down.

Pattee came in the mornings and late at night. Her sons and their wives came and went whenever they could appropriate some time. Neighbors and members of my mother's church came to say good-bye. Mother, who had been awake and talking softly from time to time during the first two days, grew increasingly lethargic and weak. Although she could not swallow, she asked for toast and fried chicken. All we could give her were liquids. She smiled when she tasted the beer we brought.

Jewelle and Jim flew in from California and spent most of their days at the hospice. A few days after I arrived, Harold joined me.

Mother's daughter-in-law, Maureen drove from South Carolina to see her, on her way to Boston. My brother's children flew in from Denver and Boston, then drove to Branford for their time with their grandmother.

As a way of communicating, those of us who were spelling each other left an informal journal on a hospital table at the foot of her bed. We noted the time, who had visited, and our observations as to whether Mother had moved, opened her eyes, attempted to say something, or breathed easily.

On the 21st the log read:

7:25 A.M.   Mom in a little distress—given meds to calm her. Pattee

5:35 P.M.   Jeff and Julie, we're going to take off—we've been here since 11 A.M. The Dr. says she will probably keep sleeping. You can reach me on my cell. Have a safe trip home. Thanks for making the journey today. I know Nana is glad that you came. Love, Shirlee and Harold

7:05 P.M.   Nana is still sleeping. Love, Jeff and Julie

On the 22nd:

8:00 A.M.   Mom sleeping peacefully. Nurse freshened her up. Reports are she is still a little tense, will be given Valium for stress, tension and breathing along with morphine (very small dose). Pattee

1:15 P.M.   We're in cafeteria. Shirlee and Harold

5:00 P.M.   We arrived at 10:30 today. Mauryne called from D.C. Bobby Hancock dropped by. We moistened Mom's lips. She had a lady visitor in red coat this A.M., no name. Mom remained "asleep" throughout the day. Shirlee and Harold

8:00 P.M.   Dropped in—Nana still sleeping peacefully. Seemingly no distress. Pattee

On the 23rd:

7:25 A.M.   Deep sleep. I did not water plants, they are moist. Mom's breathing too labored, was given a shot to help. Otherwise she seems comfortable. I don't know if she still hears me—but I told her what day etc. We think she still hears us, but close to the ear. Pattee

For the first time since we had been at the hospice, the weather turned inhospitable. Wind whipped the sound into a foaming, swirling mass. The birds were fighting the currents in the water and in the sky. High tides swamped Lovers' Island. Ravening clouds barricaded the light. Huge drops of rain attacked the windows. Darkness stayed with us all day. No one walked the grounds. Locals said the storm was a nor'easter. The only hints of cheer and warmth were the festooned fireplaces.

Mother's breathing had gotten very labored. The nurses gave her medicine that they said would help her breathing and lessen her anxiety. Fearing she would die while I was away from the room, I spent two nights at the hospice awakening to red-blue sunrises outlining the black, leafless trees.

One of those evenings, I returned to her room near midnight. The only sound was ragged breathing.

Although it was dark, a full moon on the water made the room bright near the windows. In front of the glass, three tall figures formed A-shaped silhouettes against the silver night. With their peaked baseball caps looking like bent halos, that night her grandsons had become her guardian angels. They had been waiting for me to return before they left her. Without a sound they padded out of the room.

The day before Christmas Eve, Deirdre arrived and joined me in my vigil. Melissa was on standby to leave the last days of her performance in the Disney stage presentation of *The Lion King* in Los Angeles. Her show's rules were that she could be absent only if a death occurred in her immediate family.

Jewelle and Jim returned to Palo Alto and said they would come back to Connecticut on Christmas night.

Chistmas Eve came, and with it, mild weather returned. Although we had spent the night and had gone to our house for four or five hours of sleep, I was anxious to get to the hospice. Harold and I arrived around 1:30 in the afternoon. Mother's breathing was much gentler than it had been for the last four days. Her eyes were slightly open but seemed to be watery, gray, and fixed.

Deirdre was out trying to find boxes for Christmas gifts, since none of us had done the usual shopping. Harold left to pick up some wrapping paper. He would be nearby, he said, and reachable on his cell phone. The grandsons and their wives and one girlfriend had been there earlier and had left. Pattee had made her usual early morning call. I was alone.

I held my mother's hand. It was cool but not overly so. She lay on her side turned away from the window, the water view no longer thought to be of relevance. Her bed was absolutely flat, and this was not a good sign. I had noticed that as other patients moved closer to death, the beds got lower and lower, until they were perfectly horizontal, like Mother's now. I knew she would not have preferred this position since she always liked her head to rest on at least two pillows. She said it made her sleep better.

As I gazed at my mother, hoping to will her alive with my

stare, she expressed two odd, inverse, and barely audible gulps. Twice more she breathed. Then she stopped. When her gallant heart ceased beating, she made no sound. No inelegant death rattle. No hoarse gasp. Just two lovely breaths that verged on sighs. I couldn't quite take it in. I had never seen anyone die before. Did what I think happened happen?

It was 2:35 in the afternoon. My mother did something then that she had never done in life. My mother left me holding her hand. My mother left me. My mother left. In plain sight, she eased away from me, slipping through the window, out over the lawn, over the geese, the ducks, the swans the sparrows, the squirrels, the trees, the grass, the gazebo, and the island.

The first lines of a Pueblo poem popped into my head and replayed themselves on an unbroken loop:

A long time I have lived with you
And now we must be going
Separately to be together. . . .

I found the supervising nurse just a few doors away, working on some records. "I think my mother's gone. She doesn't seem to be breathing." The nurse came to take a look. She said she saw no signs of breathing. She drew the curtains around Mother's bed and went to get another nurse with a stethoscope. The second nurse listened to my mother's chest. She confirmed that death had kept its appointment. The nurses asked me to step outside of the curtains so that they could do their final ministrations. My mother was six months and some days beyond ninety.

At a loss for what else to do, I looked out the windows. The geese were on the lawn, standing at attention again. The ducks were floating on one side of the mustache, the swans on the other. The birds and the squirrels kept to their tasks. I wondered if Mother's spirit had stopped to talk to the geese or look at the swans. I made calls to Jewelle, Pattee, Harold, Deirdre, and Melissa. I also called Althea, one of my mother's foster daughters.

I went back inside the curtain. Mother was on her back, hands joined below her waist, holding two purple blossoms from one of the plants she had been sent. Everyone seemed to know that purple was "her color." In death she looked like her Irish grandmother.

I was glad to have this time alone with her. When you are one of four siblings, time alone with a parent is precious and rare. It was my time now. I did not have to talk. She would know my thoughts. Tears came. My heart broke; time slipped and place blurred.

Harold was there within minutes, followed by Pattee and her fiancé. Pattee's oldest son, Dale, who had been a faithful companion to his grandmother, arrived with his wife. The hospice chaplain, a black man with an infectious smile and exuberant manner, said a Scripture and a prayer, and sang Harriet Tubman's favorite spiritual. Deirdre came through the door just after the prayer. Melissa called to say she was flying in with Lowell, Jewelle's son.

Early on Christmas morning, a heavy snow began. Snow fell all day. It was hard to distinguish the water from the land, the land from the white swirling flakes. For us, the holiday passed unnoticed and uncelebrated. The mourning rituals of bringing food to the home of the grieving had not yet started. By rote, we ate a dinner of leftovers at Pattee's house.

A frustrated Jewelle called to say she was stranded in Washington, D.C., because of the storm. She'd see us in the morning. Snow kept falling and dictated our quick after-dinner departure from Pattee's. Everywhere in her North Haven neighborhood, lawns glittered with bobbing reindeers, cars were parked for Christmas festivities, and families were sitting down for dinner. My mother was dead.

The child in me who loved snow and Christmas did not believe I could ever love Christmas again because Mrs. Santa Claus was dead. The person who had given me some of the best Christmases and gifts of my life would never shop again, would never whip up her special eggnog, would never bake another sweet potato pie or stuff a turkey before she cut her collard greens. She would not mix her macaroni and cheese or stir giblet gravy or fold in creamed onions. Gone. All gone. Not to be replicated by me. I would have to redefine all future Christmases, a holiday at a time.

I could not have imagined that planning my mother's funeral would be so difficult. Mother had left no particular written instructions about her service, and each of us reported the different things she had requested, often in conflicting versions. My mother's minister and our husbands acted as arbitrators.

Among the three of us, all strong women with different tastes and opinions, there was constant negotiation over most of the details. What kind of casket to choose (an elegant wood that looked like barely glazed walnut). What the obituary should say. What picture to use: whether Mother in her prime or in her old age (I wanted middle aged, my sisters wanted old, so we put an attractive older one on the front of the program and younger on the back). What Mother should wear (we all wanted her lilac-colored wedding dress, but it was much too big). Whether to keep the casket open. What kind of flowers we should order. Who should ride in the family cars, and in what order. How the processional should be lined up and what the music should be.

We took turns wearing each other down. Stress prevailed. Pattee complained of headaches; Jewelle's knee erupted into angry protest. I lost my appetite and various memories. Our childhood selves were squabbling with no Mommy to intervene. Our mother, the one who had named me after Shirley Temple and the only person who called me "Shirl," could not soothe our aches. It was our turn to be at the head of the line.

In the end, we each got something of what we felt was important to us. It was clear that we were planning our service as well as our mother's.

Six days later, on a mild winter's morning, my mother's children and grandchildren pulled together the threads and patches of her life and created a beautiful funeral quilt. Each daughter and each grandchild stood in the pulpit and, like their father and grandfather, preached about some aspect of their mother's/grandmother's exemplary life. There was laughter about her temper and feistiness; there was pride in her love of family; there was savoring of her spaghetti sauce; there was joy in the reunification of her kin; there was wonder in her love of animals; there was gladness in her compassion and generosity.

Her stepdaughter and her sons-in-law bordered the quilt with their remembrances. The music of "Danny Boy," "Abide with Me," "Precious Lord," and "Just a Closer Walk with Thee" fused together her many roots.

Mother's funeral lasted three hours, but it seemed like three minutes. Some might calculate it as one hour for each thirty years. Not exactly an equitable exchange. I did not want it to end, because I dreaded what would come next.

Her grandsons lined up by age to carry her out of the church. In death, she was surrounded by the gorgeous hues of her family's life, shading ombré tone on tone like a beautiful chiffon scarf. Among the handsome black-suited young men, a shimmer of pale canary yellow—the suit worn by my brother's eldest son, Julian III—fought its way out of the darkness and escaped like a ray of hope. A ray of joy. A special beam of light for his grandmother.

The winter sun hung low in the afternoon sky as we completed the rituals of my mother's life. Riding away from the snow-covered Beaverdale Cemetery where we left the flower-littered coffin atop the grave next to my father's headstone, I was drained and saddened. Unwillingly and without any say, I had been initiated into that sorrowful sorority of motherless daughters.

Somehow, serenity squeezed in and made a place beside sorrow in the funeral limousine. I kept telling myself that my mother died knowing she had resolved the central mystery and issue of her life. She had found her family and they had found her. She had found redemption and release. And that had made just about everything better for her. She had become a model of forbearance and forgiveness. She had become a beloved ancestor. A "MaDear" incarnate.

And I had no doubt that my mother had, at last, found grace.

Permissions

Grateful acknowledgment for permission to print selections from the following sources:

Jewelle Gibbs, James Gibbs, Dorothy Dunker, Carol Battles, Donna Dummer, Darcy Miccio Pace, Steve Hoffman, Barbara Hoffman, Julie Taylor Massey, Jeffrey Taylor, Melissa Haizlip, Deirdre Haizlip, Harold Haizlip, Dustin Suits, Linda Suits, Kenneth Scott, Madelyn Sullivan, Anna Lynch, Bernard Ruffin, Patrick Burris, Sandra Madden, Robert Washington, Deirdre Shepherd, Lisa Tolliver Burke, Thomasina Butler, Patricia Watson, John Reece McClanahan, Michael Brownstein and Gail Staggers, Ernest B. Cohen, Susan Robertson, Judith Wurtman, Alvin Rubin, Judy Huggins, Rebecca Sher, Jeannie Breslin, Jennifer J.A. Pavio, Steven Willemann, Rod Tatsuno, Georgia W. Babb, Jean Bryan, Sherry White Talbert, H. Mabel Walker, Nancy Stroud, Sharon Wyeth, Rufus J. Alexander, Vicki Surges, Arlene Mitchell, Ema Wykes, Barbara Finch, Cleo Saffoe, Wendy Quinn, Donna Iwagaki, Jess and Mary Lu Strack, Deborah Davis, Lynette Workman, James Piver, Benjamin Wilson, Patricia Watson, Bess Jones,

Frances Robb, Elizabeth Hardin, Carole Fisher, Helen Garner, Walter Barbash, Marian Philipps (M.P.) Angela DiMaria, Pam Dotson, Sarah Donnelly, Nancy Edwards, Joan Shannon, Maxine Walker, Marilyn Moe, Nancy Young, Dorothy Byrne, Donna Cooper, E. Cheely, Peggy, Kharraz, Eula Mitchell, Tom Moore, Emily Holcombe, Janice Chapin, Katouri Wilson, Tom LaSalle, Jill Smith, Christopher Lee, Hawley Fogg-Davis, Selma Gilmore, Anne Fege, M.R., Susan Talbert, Adrian Piper, Maria Root, and Margaret McIntosh.

About the Author

SHIRLEE TAYLOR HAIZLIP is a native of Connecticut. A graduate of Wellesley College, she studied urban planning at the Harvard Graduate School of Design. She also worked as a teaching fellow in sociology at Tufts University. After living half of her life on the East Coast, she lived for eight years in the U.S. Virgin Islands. She returned to New York and Connecticut and is now settled in Los Angeles with her husband. The mother of two Yale-educated daughters, she is the author of *The Sweeter the Juice.*